How to Hear the Voice of God

By: COLETTE TOACH

AMI BOOKSHOP

www.ami-bookshop.com

How to Hear the Voice of God

ISBN-10: 1626640319
ISBN-13: 978-1-62664-031-3

1st Printing August 2014

Published by **AMI Bookshop**
E-mail Address: admin@ami-bookshop.com
Web Address: www.ami-bookshop.com

Scripture quotations are taken from the Apostolic Movement International (AMIV) version of the Bible.

Contents

Your Christian Foundation

Introduction – Your Christian Foundation

We had a very interesting experience a couple of years back. My father kept having a problem with his front door. Every time he closed it, the thing would get stuck. So Craig, my husband (and our handyman) came with his bag of tools and a wood plane. He started by taking the door off its hinges.

Then he sanded it, planed it and then fitted the door back in correctly. It was a perfect fit. It worked beautifully... for the first two minutes!

After we had opened and closed the door a few times, it got stuck again. So once again, he took the door off the hinges, sanded it, planed it down, fitted it and measured it.

He is very analytical. So trust me when I say, he did a very good job and took a very long time. After doing this for the first few swings it was fine, but then it got stuck again. He sat there thinking, "What am I doing wrong?"

I was standing on the inside of the house and he was on the outside. Suddenly, I looked to the side of the doorpost and I saw a huge crack in the wall next to the doorframe. In fact, the crack was so big I could see right through the wall to the outside where Craig was standing!

I peeked around and said, "Craig, I think we just found our problem. "

You see, the wall had started to split and was pushing the door post skew. The foundation of the house had started to sink and those walls were starting to pull apart. Needless to say… they moved.

Building a Strong House

Many Christians have a house that looks like this: It has cracks and it does not have a solid foundation. You are trying to learn how to bring it all together and I am here today to help you do that.

I am here not just to show you how to build a solid foundation, but to show you how to build a solid house as well.

How do you build this house, so that you do not have cracks in your walls? How do you build this house correctly, so that you are doing what God wants you to do?

I am going to teach you how to hear God very clearly, in different ways. By the time you have applied these three principles, you will never ask yourself this question again, "What is God's will for my life? What has God called me to do?"

You will know what God's will is for your life right now. From hearing Him through the Urim and Thummim to seeing His plan for you in the Word, you will realize that the Lord has been speaking to you all along. All you need to do now is to learn how to listen!

Hearing God Through the Word

Chapter 01 – Hearing God Through the Word

If you want to build a good, solid wall you need three elements. One of the first elements you need is cement. Without cement nothing comes together. The Word of God is that cement.

Have you ever been to a building site? They have big bags of cement powder piled up all over the place. It is hard and strong. It is the foundation of everything. It is this cement that will help to bring together everything that God told you.

Have you ever sat next to someone in church and they said, "I was studying the Word and God told me 'this' and 'that'?" Then you ask, "How did God tell you? Did you see a scripture that said, 'Thus saith the Lord'?"

I grew up hearing all the time that the Word is God's voice speaking to me. You go to church and they say, "You need to read the Word. The Bible is the voice and word of God. If you read the Bible, you will know what to do for your life."

So you read the Bible and think, "Who cares about Noah? Who cares about Gideon? Right now, I am having marital problems. Right now, I have a conflict in my life. Right now, I need to know if I need to move across the country.

Maybe I can relate to Abraham because he had to move across the country like I do now. "Yet Lord, how do I hear your voice through your Word?"

It just seems sometimes, that you are reading a bunch of stories. You do not know how to take those stories and principles and how to apply them to your modern day life right here and now. If that is how you feel, then I am here to help you out.

1. Understanding the Language of the Word

The first thing you need to do when you are reading the Word is to feed pictures into your mind. You keep looking at the Word of God as just words. Since the beginning of time, God spoke in types and shadows.

Even when Jesus walked the earth what did He use when He spoke? Parables. Why do you think that is? It is because we understand pictures.

I bet you can remember the last movie you watched more than the last sermon you heard. (Unless it was one of mine, in which I painted pictures of course!) I shared my story of the house with the crack in the wall, and so you are going to remember those pictures.

Somewhere along your walk, that picture is going to come to your mind and you will say, "Lord, what are you telling me here?" He will use that picture.

If you want to understand the language of the Word, do not think it is about what version of the Bible you are reading. You have to understand that it is a language of pictures. You need to learn to visualize the Word.

When you start reading the Scriptures, visualize what is going on in the scripture as you are reading it. Picture yourself right there in that situation.

You have Paul giving a long sermon late into the middle of the night. Can you see yourself huddled there in the upper room? It is late and everyone is yawning. Can you imagine the guy sitting on the window and thinking, "Hmm, that looks a bit dangerous"?

As Paul drones on, the guy falls asleep and falls out of the window. You hear this big "thud" and realize that the guy fell out of the window and killed himself. Can you imagine the panic?

Can you imagine being in a church meeting where someone sitting on the church window dozes off, falls and wipes himself out?

See Yourself There

Then can you see yourself rushing outside with the crowd? You arrive and watch as Paul raises the dead boy up. I bet you will never forget that scripture now.

You see, it is not enough to just picture the Word, but you have to see yourself there.

Something happens when you put yourself in the Word. You feel the emotion of it. What you are doing is using your entire soul. You are bringing your soul into subjection to the Word. You are not just seeing or understanding the Word, you are feeling the Word.

When you do that, the Word becomes alive to you. Jesus is manifested in the Word. The Word is alive. It is living. You can feel it. You can experience, taste and smell it.

Can you see Peter walking to the temple after the day of Pentecost? Can you hear the hustle and bustle of the marketplace? Can you smell the scent of someone cooking as Peter walks by?

It was dirty and messy. There was a crippled guy on the side of the road. He is grubby and begging. Peter stops and says, "Silver and gold have I none, but what I have I will give to you." You are there. You see that man leap and walk.

Maybe he did not have all his teeth but he had a big, gummy smile. He is leaping and praising God. Everyone that saw it was so excited and they danced all the way to the temple. Wow, I am so excited visualizing this. I want to go raise somebody up right now!

See? God is speaking to you through the Word. It is not good enough to say, "I read my chapter of the Word today." No, you must see yourself in it. Numbers and Leviticus are books that I love. I can picture them.

It says, if this happens, do this. I can see this poor guy coming with a problem to the priests and the priests say, "You must go back and for seven days do this and this."

It gives me a picture of what it must have been like to live in that day and age under those laws. Imagine having to live by those guidelines and rules. It gives me a picture and an understanding of where these people came from.

However, if you are just reading the Word with your head or your own understanding, the Lord will not speak to you through it, because the Lord speaks in pictures. So, every time you read the Scriptures - visualize them.

Make a Movie

We are in a modern age where there are videos everywhere. So make a video in your mind. Say to yourself, "If I had to make a movie of this chapter, how would I project it? Who would act in the main part? What part would I play in the movie? How would that person react?"

Feed the Word into your spirit using all five senses. Was it cold? Was it hot? Suddenly, the Word is not a scripture that you have to read like the law. It is not just boring stuff. It is now living, powerful and sharper than any two-edged sword.

However, it will not become powerful or living until you make it so. Let me tell you something - the devil knows the Bible better than you. So you would think he would be born again by now wouldn't you?

There are lots of people who have read the Word, but do not know the power of it because they do not feed it into their spirit. How do you feed something into your spirit? The same way you get something out of your spirit - through your five senses.

Using Your Five Senses

You get it through what you see, taste, smell, touch and hear. That is how we get things out of our spirits as well as how it goes in.

You know what is exciting about doing this? You will go to the Lord in prayer or be traveling on the road and have a problem, when suddenly the Lord presses rewind and play.

Suddenly the movie that you pushed into your spirit a year ago will pop up into your mind and you will think, "Why am I thinking about that right now?"

Guess what? The Lord just spoke to you through His Word. You are waiting for the "Thus saith the Lord" message word for word. People have the idea that they will wake up and the Lord will say, "Go to Psalm chapter 2 verse 3. "

Then they will have to go quickly and look through the Word. "What is God telling me?"

No, that is not what it means to hear God through the Word. So, if you are not getting that kind of clear revelation, you can chill because you are normal like the rest of us.

I am not saying God does not use it that way. I am sure He does, but He mostly speaks in pictures. Why do you think the Word is so pictorial? Why do you think it is so full of stories and illustrations? Why do you think it gives brutally honest images sometimes?

Some of the pictures are really "way out there". Read the Song of Solomon. There is nothing left hidden there. The Lord was trying to show us, even in that book, how He speaks.

Solomon did not just walk up to his bride and say, "I love you."

He said, "You are as beautiful as… "

"Your hair is as lovely as a flock of goats."

(This apparently was a compliment in that age. But in our modern era… not so much.)

The point is - he painted pictures. The Lord speaks in pictures. Start to read the Word in pictures and as you push them down, eventually they will come back up again.

Faith comes by hearing, and hearing, by the rhema word of God. First you have to push those words into your spirit, and then, once those pictures come back out, faith is formed, because it comes out as rhema.

The Word Will Come out as Rhema

It may only go in as Logos or even just as your imagination. You may not even feel any anointing on it at first. However, when that word comes out, it will come out as rhema. It comes in power, in the right place and at the right time.

Have you ever experienced this in your walk before? You listened to a message or read a book but didn't really get anything out of it at the time.

Then somewhere along the road, something happens and you say, "You know, this situation reminds me of a story I read. It reminds me of something that 'that' preacher shared with me."

The Lord just spoke to you. This is a powerful way to hear the voice of the Lord, and you are neglecting it. Now, let me get to the next point, otherwise I will carry on with this because it is my favorite way to hear the voice of God. I am sure you can tell. Make the Word fun. Make it alive in you and let God speak to you.

2. Reading the Word With Intent

Now, the next thing you can do to hear God's voice through the Word is to read it with intent. In other words, read until something hits you.

It means to read deliberately or on purpose and for a specific reason. Say for example that you have a need. You are battling with bitterness, lust or you are having a conflict with someone.

Pick up the Word with that question in your mind. Read the Word and expect to find the answer there. Now, you might not always find the answer in the first scripture or two.

When I have put out my faith and said, "Lord, I really need a solution for this particular problem. I really need a direct answer for this counseling crisis. Lord, I need something more than a vision. I need something solid that I can stand on and confess."

I pick up the Word and start reading with the question in my mind of, "Lord, how do I deal with this problem?" I will start reading and reading. I will swap through several books of the Bible.

I will go from chapter to chapter and I will let my eyes skim the pages until suddenly the right verse will hit me at the right time. It will be the exact answer to my problem.

Read in Faith

Now, the key to that one is firstly to read in faith and to put the question in your mind. So many people get the impression that if God wanted to say something to them, He would just jump out and say it.

So they read the Word thinking, "Okay God, say something to me." Well, that is not a very nice conversation. When I have a conversation with someone, it is a "permission conversation."

I ask you something and then you ask me something. I do not just walk up to someone and tell them what I want them to do. Unless, of course, I have not had my first cup of coffee that morning and I am in the mood to boss someone around... but that is something completely different!

The Lord is not going to do that though. He is not going to impose His Word on you. You will not be walking along when suddenly He comes and jumps on you, or shouts at you. He is not that kind of God. He is a loving, tender God.

He wants to converse back and forward with you. So, when you come to Him with a question, He is going to give you the answer. Now, when you read the Word this way, it can take up a bit of time.

The more you get used to flowing this way, the quicker you will find the right scripture at the right time. When you do find it, that scripture will become an anchor point in your life.

Discovering Keynote Scriptures for Life

I remember one time when I was battling with a huge attack on my mind. I did not know what it was. My dreams were full of nightmares and while I was going through the day, terrible thoughts would run through my mind.

It was a battlefield in my mind. I took authority, I prayed and I struggled. I said, "Lord, you have to help me." I started reading through the Word and I came to the scripture about casting down imaginations and every high thing that exalts itself above the glory of God and bringing every thought into captivity to the obedience of Christ. (2 Cor 10:5)

Wow! That set me on fire. I said, "That is it! That is my answer!" Then I said, "Satan, you loose your hold because I bring into captivity every thought right now!"

I am very pictorial, so I saw all those thoughts out there. I grabbed them, put them in prison and brought them to captivity under Christ, and God had the key. Then just like that, I was free.

Every time I had one of those thoughts again, that scripture came to mind and I brought those thoughts into captivity like snatching birds from the air and putting them in a cage. I grabbed them and put them under the Lord. After that, I stopped having attacks on my mind.

It took the Word to give me that kind of power. I needed that anchor. When you read the Word of God with intent, you will get the kind of scriptures that become keynotes in your life. They will become pillars in your life that keep you anchored.

Guess what? You just heard from God. You keep thinking that hearing from God in this way is this super-duper thing that only high-level apostles can do. If that was the case, then why did the Lord take the time to put the together in the first place?

You are already hearing from the Lord. You just need to identify it. You need to practice hearing Him in this way.

3. Forming new Templates Through Memorization

Now the final way to hear the Lord through the Scriptures is to form new templates. You need to form new molds in your mind for success and blessing. There is no easy way around this. It takes a little work. It takes some memorization of Scripture.

It is a lot like reading the Word and making a movie out of it like I said earlier. You need to do that deliberately with specific scriptures. The scripture you use will depend on what you are struggling with.

Maybe you are at a point in your life where you want to understand doctrine or are trying to figure out your calling. Maybe, you are battling with sin in your life or struggling with finances.

Step 1: Read With Intent

Begin by reading the Word with intent. As you do this, scriptures are going to pop up and when they do, write them down.

Step 2: Memorize Scriptures That Pop Up

Then, after you write the scriptures down, start to memorize them.

Step 3: Visualize the Scripture as You Memorize It

As you memorize that scripture, make a movie of it in your mind and see yourself in it. Say it again and again. Continue to push it into your spirit.

Perhaps the scripture you were memorizing was,

Mark 11:23

> *For assuredly I say to you, That whoever will say to this mountain, Be removed, and be cast into the sea; and will not doubt in his heart, but will believe that those things that he says will come to pass; he will have whatever he says. (AMIV)*

Each time you quoted it, you envisioned that mountain being thrown into the sea.

The next time you are in prayer you say, "Lord, what did I do? Where did I go wrong? What has happened?" Suddenly, the picture of the mountain that you were pushing into your spirit will come to your mind.

What is the Lord saying? The verse said that, "Whoever says to this mountain be removed... "

He is saying, "Remove the mountain." You just heard the voice of God through the Word.

Do you see why pictures are so important? If you are not using the Word as your cement, you are going to find a nice big crack in your wall, because if the pictures are not based on the Word, then what are they based on?

What Are You Basing Your Pictures On?

Think about all the pictures you pushed into your spirit within the last 48 hours. I guarantee the pictures came from books you read, conversations you had or movies you watched.

What pictures are you pushing into your spirit? What are you giving God to work with? What cement does He have to build your house with? If you do not learn to hear God from the Word first, then learning to hear God in the next two ways will not make any sense to you.

Cement comes first. The Word is our basis and our foundation. Once you can hear God through the Word, the next step, which is hearing God through the spirit, becomes so much easier.

Hearing God Through the Urim and Thummim

Chapter 02 – Hearing God Through the Urim and Thummim

In this day and age everyone is quite amazed by the gifts of the Spirit. I am not knocking the gifts - I love them. In fact, we have a couple of schools with teaching on them. However, if you do not go to the Word first, you will not have a solid base.

Do you know why? It is because the Spirit is like water. When you get cement in those big bags, you have to mix it with the water. Then the cement sets. You need the two together, side by side.

I see such an imbalance in the Church. I see people with bags and bags of cement, thinking that cement alone will build them a house. Then on the opposite extreme, I see believers with jugs and jugs of water who think that water alone will build them a house.

The Spirit of God Activates the Word

You need the Spirit of God to activate the knowledge of the Word. Only then, will you get wisdom out of it. However, if you do not have enough Word in you, what is the Spirit going to activate? Nothing!

You will just get into deception because you will base all of your decisions on feelings, impressions, impulses and good ideas, instead of on the scriptures you have pushed into your spirit.

Also, when that picture comes out, is it a picture that you pushed in using the Scripture? Or is the picture that comes out based on something you got from the world, which can be manipulated by the enemy way too easily?

Find the Balance

You have two imbalances. The first imbalanced view says, "All you need is the Word, the Word, the Word!"

I don't know about you, but I have never seen anyone build a house with cement bags. Especially not a secure house, because without water, cement can be blown away like dust.

However, if you take some water and mix that in, something starts to happen. A reaction takes place. The cement can set and become so solid and hard, that it will not crack.

If you are imbalanced on either side, then you are like the house that had a big crack in the wall. Why? It is because the cement could not take the pressure - it was not mixed right. Something went wrong. The balance was all wrong.

We have a lot of teaching already on hearing God through the spirit. Now it is great to hear Him through the spirit, but if you are just going on the Spirit alone and have no Word in you, what is being activated?

You may have a rock on which to build the house, which is Jesus Christ. However, you have no house. We are the temples of the Holy Ghost. If we want to be a solid house on the rock, we need to build with the proper amount of cement and water.

Revelation always confirms the Word. Do not think you can do it on the Word alone, because water brings life. Water activates.

The Word is like this handful of knowledge that may just be a sand-like substance, but you just need to add a little water to that knowledge and you will get wisdom out of it.

Using Principles Effectively

So many people say to me, "How do you know when to apply what principle?" After they have gone through the teachings and books they wonder, "When do I know the correct time to apply specific principles?"

"It seems that there is so much that I have to keep in my head." It's good that you have all that knowledge, but it takes wisdom to make that knowledge work. The Spirit of God is the only thing that can bring that kind of reaction in your life.

If you are not finding any wisdom, then you are too dry. All you have is principles, principles and more principles! On the other hand, if you do not have anything solid and you keep being swayed by your emotions, then you are just water, water and more water.

God Wants to Converse With You!

It is not so complicated. Hearing His voice is the inheritance of every child of God. What is the first thing that parents do when a baby is born? They take the baby in their arms and start making the most ridiculous noises that you have ever heard.

They start talking to the child right away. Even before it is born, they talk to the baby while it is in the belly. If we as natural parents cuddle and speak to our babies to let them know that we are there, then how much more our heavenly Father?

You think you have to earn the right to hear His voice or somehow be spiritual and righteous enough before He will tell you His great will. No, He is making those "coochie coo" sounds to you all the time. You are just not listening.

He is a loving and tender father. He is speaking. He is giving you impressions. He is letting pictures from the Word pop up in your mind all the time. You think, "What am I thinking about that for? That was stupid."

Hello...? The Lord is talking to you! It is so simple. Then after you learn to hear the impressions in your spirit, the next things to flow in, are visions and journaling. These two go hand in hand. First though let us dig into the easiest way to hear His voice – through your spiritual Urim and Thummim

The Urim and Thummim

> *1 Samuel 28:6* *And when Saul enquired of the LORD [Yahweh], the LORD [Yahweh] did not answer him, either by dreams, or by Urim, or by prophets.*

There is nothing more damaging in a family than when parents play favorites. I know I have personally worked with a lot of people who had this experience growing up and it can really mess you up.

It messes with your whole perception of life and of relationships and even your view of marriage. It can destroy somebody's life.

Unfortunately, it is a sad truth that in the church there are many believers walking around who had parents who played favorites. And when you are not the favorite, you grow up with the idea that there are some people in this world who are special and who have things handed to them and then... there are the rest of us.

We are the ones that have to work hard to get what we want in life.

The problem with this kind of upbringing is that you start to view God in this way too. You start to think that God has favorites.

When it comes to hearing God's voice, you can get yourself so whelmed and frustrated. You can find yourself trying so hard to just hear from Him, to just get some of His attention that you miss one important fact.

Here is an important fact to remember: Your Heavenly Father is not like your natural father.

You don't have to be a little child pulling at his pant leg saying, "Daddy, look at me." Trying to shout, trying to scream, trying to just get His attention.

Your heavenly father is not like that. In fact, He is the kind of parent, that when you are ignoring Him, rejecting Him and running your own way, He runs after you to get your attention.

When you least expect it, you turn to find Him reaching down to pick you up and to give you love you did not deserve.

God Wants to Speak to You

However, you have this image of the Lord that is based on your relationship with your natural father; on your upbringing, and on how you have been programmed to view the world. And this thinking says, "God gives revelation to some and not others. The heavenly father speaks to some and not others."

Now, one thing I want to smash is that entire wrong concept. Our Father does not speak to some and not the others. He is not a father that will just have a conversation with one child and not speak to the other.

He wants to speak to you. He wants to communicate with you. This is the first conviction that you need to get, when coming to hear God's voice.

Not only does He want to speak to you, but He is already speaking to you all of the time!

You don't need to keep trying so hard. The truth is that it is your very trying and striving that is blocking the voice of God in your life.

The reason why you are not hearing Him is that you are so busy running around trying to get His attention that you don't hear or don't see the obvious that is right in front of you.

There is a big thrust in the Church concerning prophetic revelation. There is a lot of emphasis being placed on the gifts and on getting revelation for others.

Now, that's fantastic and the body of Christ needs it - but until you can come to a place where you can hear His voice for yourself, what do you have to give out to others?

Only Hearing for Others Is not Good Enough

Now, perhaps you have learned to minister to others and to get revelation on their behalf. Unfortunately though when it comes to your personal life, it feels like you always fall short of the mark.

You feel that you are not spiritual or holy enough for God to speak to you about your own life.

Here is a vital fact to remember: The day you became born again, you became as holy and righteous as Jesus Christ because you stand in His blood.

When you stand in Christ and the Father looks down at you, do you know what He sees? He sees the blood of Christ and that cleanses you from all sin and all unrighteousness and you stand as perfect before His eyes just as Jesus Christ Himself is sinless and pure. (Go read 1 John 1 for a confirmation on that)

He looks upon you with love, and He wants to give and He wants to speak to you. If you can get that conviction, then you are well on your way to begin hearing the voice of God for yourself.

If you can stop the striving for a moment, you might come to realize that He has been talking to you all along.

You have been so busy running around, while all along the Lord has been standing right by your side saying, "Hello... I have been standing here all along. If you would just be quiet and come and listen, you will hear my voice."

Expect the Unexpected

Perhaps the way you are hearing God's voice is not what you expected. That is what this particular book and certainly these first few chapters are about. They are all about teaching you how to identify the Lord's voice in your life.

I am not even going to go on to sharing with others until you have learned to master this in your own life. We are going to go into the practical stuff on ministering to others soon enough, but for now I want you to identify the fact that God has been speaking to you.

By the end of this chapter you are going to jump up and down and say, "I have been hearing His voice!

Once you get that conviction and once you start seeing that, your spiritual life is going to take off in a hundred directions because God hasn't been silent. God hasn't been ignoring you. God does not have favorites.

What the Urim and Thummim Is

> *Exodus 28:30 And you will put in the breastplate of judgment the **urim** and the Thummim; and they will be upon Aaron's heart, when he goes in before the LORD [Yahweh...*

In the Old Testament the Lord had Moses make a very special robe for Aaron to wear during his office. By far the most fascinating part of it was the breastplate. You can read all the details of it in Exodus 28, but I want to draw your attention to the Urim and Thummim that is mentioned.

Tradition suggests that they were two smooth stones –
one being black and the other white. So depending on
which one Aaron pulled out, would give you the direct
answer from God that you wanted.

You will see this mentioned a number of times in the Old
Testament and it was a wonderful way for the children of
Israel to get a direct answer from the Lord. When they
needed a "yes" or "no" answer about something, they
would pay Aaron and visit and he would slip his hand into
his breastplate and pull out either the "Urim" or the
"Thummim."

Getting a Urim from the Lord said "yes" and a Thummim
said "no"! Wouldn't it be nice to have a set of these stones
hanging around in your sock draw for emergencies? Well,
the good news is that we have something way better than
that.

From the time the Holy Spirit came to dwell inside of you,
He brought along His Urim and Thummim and deposited
them directly into your spirit. Aaron wore the stones over
his heart – a symbol of what we now have through Christ.
An inheritance inside our own hearts!

> **Ephesians 6:14** *Stand therefore, having your loins
> girded about with truth, and having on the **breastplate**
> of righteousness*

Today every believer gets to wear the breastplate! With the indwelling of the Holy Spirit comes the ability to get a straight answer from the Lord.

Relating It to the Urim and Thummim

This is how the Urim and Thummim works. It is simply God speaking through your spirit and influencing the emotions in your soul. (For more detail on this please read the Prophetic Functions book)

The Lord specifically speaks through the "emotion function" of your soul when giving you a Urim or Thummim. When He speaks to you in this way, you will experience a deep gut feeling of "YES!" or one of "NO!"

Just think back on some life changing experiences. I guarantee that during these times you either had a deep sense of peace or a deep sense of foreboding. Well, that was your Urim and Thummim talking there.

The Lord was giving you the "yes/no" answer you were looking for. In fact, once you make it a practice to listen to the influence of your spirit more often, you will come to realize that you get these deep feelings throughout your day.

Listening to Your Spirit

The key with the Urim and Thummim is really to be sensitive to the spirit. I think that we tend to run ahead of the Lord sometimes.

Our mind gets in the way, and we get an idea of what we should be doing. Before the Lord has had a chance to speak to us we are off... we are doing, making and we are changing the world... It is only when we hit that big fat wall that we come to realize, "Actually, I should have listened to my spirit."

This is something that you should really be developing on a daily basis. What is fantastic about the spiritual Urim and Thummim is that this is something that you can do 24 hours a day because the Holy Spirit is speaking 24 hours a day.

He is telling you where to go and what direction to take in every part of your life.

Don't sit and wait for the Urim and Thummim only when you are ministering or when you specifically need direction. What I want you to begin now is to be aware of the Urim and Thummim in your spirit all of the time for every decision that you are making.

Let's look at some practical places where you will use the Urim and Thummim.

Intercession

Let's look at prayer.

You get big "prayer warriors" that spend more time making a prayer list than they do in prayer. They make their list so long that just reading through it casually takes an hour.

They rush into prayer, with every intent of storming the gates of heaven and to break down the gates of hell.

I can imagine the Lord standing there thinking, "Wow, that looks quite intense. I wonder if they will allow me to get a word in there...?" Half of the time what you are praying and the burdens you were praying for are not even of the Lord.

He should not need to shout from the heavens and say, "You are praying in the wrong direction." If you just stopped for a minute to hear what your spirit is saying you would know if you are praying right or not.

So before you arm yourself to attack every demon in hell and to bring every person on your list before God, ask yourself, "Do I feel a Urim or do I feel a Thummim on this?"

I want you to try this the next time you pray. When you come to pray in intercession and you have someone that has asked you to pray for them, ask yourself, "What do I sense in my spirit?"

 Do you feel, "yeah, yeah, now is the time to pray" or do you feel, "Hm, the time is not yet"?

If you feel a Urim in intercession the words will tumble out of your mouth effortlessly. If it is a Thummim, you will feel like it is stopped up with cotton wool!

Why would the Lord give you a Thummim? Perhaps the circumstances are not right; perhaps your faith is not strong enough; perhaps that person's faith is not at that place yet.

Learn to listen to your spirit. Learn to know when you are going in the right direction and when you are going in the wrong direction.

Experiencing the Thummim

You know, so often I have come to the Lord in prayer, even with emergency situations. "Lord, we have this financial crisis or we have this health crisis." You come to pray and you feel as if there is a cotton wool in your mouth. You just can't seem to find your words.

You feel like you are hitting a wall in the spirit. When this happens, the Lord is saying, "Not now."

"But Lord, this is an emergency situation here!"

"Not now. Now is not the time."

Now if you push through and ignore the warning bells, all you are doing is just speaking empty words. I promise you are going to feel exhausted in the end.

Experiencing the Urim

Then there will be a time when you are in prayer and a thought will pop up in your mind. You might see a vision of someone you know, so you will just casually hold them up praying, "Lord, I just want to bless my sister there..."

Then "bam" you feel a waterfall starting to flow out of your belly! You just know that you are praying in the right direction. The next thing you know you feel charged with electricity!

Revelation flows, decrees come forth and the anointing comes down!

Now, wouldn't it be exciting if every time you prayed, you prayed with power and you had that excitement? Well, if you are praying in God's will and if you are praying in His direction you will always feel that power.

Prayer should revive and invigorate you. If you keep coming away exhausted, you are not listening to your Urim and Thummim.

You are not listening to the direction of the Lord and even worse, if you are praying in the wrong direction you could even come under a backlash.

Daily Life

God wants to be involved in every part of your life. He wants to be involved in your daily decision-making and this is another aspect where you can use the Urim and Thummim.

 "Lord, should I pay this bill or that one?"

"Lord, should I move to this town or that one?"

Is this trivial? Absolutely, but if you are with your spouse or your friend, is it trivial to say, "What do you think, we should do? Should we go here or there?"

So if you can ask that of your spouse or a friend, then why not the Lord? Is He not your bridegroom? Is He not your friend?

If you just start integrating the Lord into every area of your life and taking His voice seriously, you are going to start experiencing Him in a whole new way.

You are going to see the Lord move in your life. You will no longer just know of Him or just understand the principles, but you will come to know Him in a very intimate way.

Make the Lord a part of your decision making, wherever you go this week and whatever decision you make.

Okay, also have some balance here. This is not a license to get paranoid. Don't be afraid now to make a step because you didn't hear a Urim or Thummim!

I am not saying that you should go extreme, I am just saying that you should become sensitive to what you hear in your spirit.

Start involving the Lord in every part of your life and listen to your spirit. Listen before you run off in one of your hundred directions. There is not always time to sit down and journal and get a complicated answer from the Lord. (We will look at journaling later.)

No matter how many other ways you will learn to hear the voice of God, the Urim and Thummim will remain with you always.

Hearing God Through Dreams

Chapter 03 – Hearing God Through Dreams

> *Job 33:15 In a dream, in a vision of the night, when deep sleep falls upon men, in slumberings upon the bed;*

This is common to many believers and also the next easiest way to hear God's voice (if you know how to interpret them of course!)

Once you have mastered dream interpretation, you should then move on from there and develop every other way of hearing from God.

Moving Into Dreams

Like I said before, variety is the spice of life. Let's hear from the Lord in every way possible and if you don't flow in dreams yet, desire it.

Allow the Lord to speak to you in dreams - you know, you might start enjoying your sleep more. It is a fantastic way to hear from the Lord. I am hoping to bring balance by saying to not rely only on one way of hearing from the Lord. Learn to develop all of them.

Understanding Dreams

With that being said, I am going to give you the gist of the main points of dream interpretation. If you have already read my book The Way of Dreams and Visions then you can skip this part and move straight on to the next chapter.

If not... dig in and allow the Holy Spirit to put some things into perspective for you.

The biggest mistake most people make when trying to interpret dreams is to assume that everything and everyone they dream about represents that very thing/person.

Key Principle

The most important principle to remember is that most of the dreams you have fall into a category called, "internal dreams." This means that every person, place and object in that dream is a representation of a part of your own life.

So if you dream that your sister-in-law has a baby, please do not bash down her door to tell her the good news! Your dreams are a picture of yourself! Your sister-in-law represents a part of yourself, as does that baby.

Understanding the Parables

The Word is full of types and shadows. The Lord Jesus Himself spoke only in parables.

In the same way, your dreams are like parables – the Lord is telling you a story to get His message across to you. In the same way that Jesus' parables had deeper meanings, so do your dreams.

Now had Jesus told everyone the parable of the Good Samaritan, it would have been odd for someone in the crowd to rush out and try to find the real man Jesus was talking about.

No, the parable was clear. Jesus was telling a story - using pictures they could relate to - to get a message across to them. The same holds true for your dreams. The Lord is using pictures that are common to you and to the Word to give you a message.

The first place to begin in understanding your dreams is to categorize them. Before I jump into that though, I want to look at why God gives you dreams in the first place – especially as a prophet.

What is the purpose of it all? Then more importantly, once you have interpreted a dream what are you supposed to do with it? Well, here are some of the main purposes for receiving a dream from the Lord.

4 Steps to Dream Interpretation

Step 1: Categorizing Your Dreams

Before you can begin to understand what the characters represent to you in your dreams, it is a good idea to categorize them. You need to identify if the dream is a healing, internal, prophetic or just a garbage dream.

Once you have identified that the dream is internal or prophetic, write it down and move on to step 2.

Here are some hints on how to identify which category the dream falls into.

a. Prophetic

A prophetic dream is very clear. It is a short, clear dream with a single message. Often you will have a few short dreams one after the other, each having a similar message.

The most outstanding aspect of a prophetic dream is that you are not a participant. In dreams like this, you will find yourself standing on the outside and watching the events.

This kind of dream concerns future events. It functions like the word of wisdom and needs to be used discerningly. Daniel is a prime example of this. He received external prophetic dreams with regards to Israel and the empires of his time. His dreams always had a future orientation.

Joseph also interpreted the King of Egypt's external dream, which allowed him to save many lives, even the lives of his nation. Note how even external dreams were given in symbolism. Even in an external dream the characters may not be who they are in real life.

b. Healing

In a healing dream you will most likely relive past events. You may find yourself saying things in your dream you wish you had said in that particular circumstance.

Perhaps you will go back to past houses, events or time frames in your life and re-experience an event, but this time with a happy ending.

If you have a dream in which you seem to be running or hiding but then finally stop to confront that which is chasing you, you are having a healing dream.

All of these things are very characteristic of a healing dream. You might even wake up crying or laughing after a dream like this.

c. Garbage Dream

A dream that is over complicated with many changes of scenery and events is very likely to just be your inner man "throwing out" the junk it had accumulated for that day.

You will most likely have many garbage dreams if you get more into the Word and spend time with the Lord, because your mind will be making space for the Word and will "throw out" the garbage you have stored in there for years.

A dream, where you display emotions and characteristics that are not natural to you, are simply your sub-conscious "living out" those feelings and hidden temptations that you experienced during the day. These dreams are simply purging dreams and do not have an interpretation.

d. Internal and Internal Prophetic Dreams

The most outstanding aspect of an internal dream is that you are the "star of the show."

Next to garbage dreams, this dream type will be the most common you will experience.

Sometimes they will simply be a picture of what is going on in your spirit right now, although as a prophet you will receive a lot of direction for the future in these kinds of dreams.

So in identifying if your dream falls under the "internal dreams" category, ask yourself, "Was I the main star?"

If that is the case the dream is internal and the characters symbolic of something within yourself.

An internal dream will often give you direction for your spiritual life. It functions the same way as a word of knowledge, in that it relates to you those things of the past and present.

An internal dream always speaks of your spiritual life. It will let you know if you have gotten off the path, or if you need to be placing more emphasis on something. It will give you an idea of what state your spirit is in and if there is something lacking in your life.

It may also tell you when you have birthed something new or have come to a place of rest or promotion.

The Internal Prophetic Dream

An internal dream has a slightly different emphasis. Joseph is a good example of this. When the Lord gave him the dreams of his brothers' sheaves bowing to his sheaf, indicating that his family would one day, bow before him.

These dreams were internal because they concerned him personally, but yet they were also prophetic in that they were giving him a word for the future.

Another good example would be the dreams of the baker and butler. Joseph interpreted those dreams in prison. (Genesis 40:5) Both concerned them personally, but also gave a prophetic word of what was going to happen.

Internal prophetic dreams function the same way as a word of wisdom, only that the word pertains to you personally. The symbols in your dream represent a part of yourself.

STEP 2: Sensing the Spirit

Next, sense the spirit on the dream. Was there a negative or a positive spirit? Was there a spirit of peace, joy, fear, death, life, change or insecurity? This step is more relevant than you realize!

This point is applicable to both dreams and visions!

The spirit of the dream can change the interpretation completely.

Consider the vision that Peter had of the blanket being lowered with all the unclean animals.

You would expect the connotation of this vision to be negative, but in fact it was positive. Eating the unclean animals was portrayed as a good thing. The Lord was trying to tell Peter that what He considered unclean (the Gentiles) God had also cleansed by His blood.

Now what if the vision had been negative? If this vision was a warning, it could well have meant that Peter was being tempted to partake in something unclean and that he should avoid it. Can you see how the positive/negative orientation of a dream or vision can change the interpretation entirely?

So consider your dream. Once you have it categorized, ask yourself, "Did this dream feel good or bad? Did I feel positive or negative?"

STEP 3: Identifying the Symbols

This is where you are going to break the dream down and "dissect" it. Once you become more accustomed to dream interpretation you will not need to break the dream down as much as you will see the interpretation without having to "dig through" all the details.

But for those who are still trying their hand at dream interpretation this is a good way to go until you learn how to flow better in the spirit.

Make yourself a list with the letters A – F. Then under each letter, list the corresponding place, scene, character, object, creature and color as they appear in the dream. Reading through the helps that I list below, systematically identify the symbol for each of these points one by one.

Now is a good time to mention that I cover all of the symbols here in more detail in my Dreams and Visions Symbol Dictionary.

A: Places

Make a list of the various places encountered in the dream. Often you may dream of places that are familiar to you. It could be that a time of healing is being brought to that period of your life or that the Lord is exposing something that happened during that time.

Churches can speak of a place of worship. If it is an old style church, it could be speaking of the religious, status quo system. A house could speak of your life, your body as a temple of the Holy Spirit.

Places such as monuments or historical buildings may speak of things relating to the past - things gone by.

You might find yourself running through alleyways or dark streets. This often speaks of running blind and not having direction. If the feeling that comes with the place is negative and fearful, it could be that the Lord is revealing to you that the enemy is wreaking havoc in your life and sending you running in all sorts of directions - none of which are of the Lord.

Of course if you find yourself in a meadow where the sun is shining and you feel peace, the Lord could be revealing to you that you have entered into a time of rest and peace with Him. This could speak of a time of freedom and escape from the pressure around you.

Each of these would have a specific meaning pertaining to you as an individual. Look to the Lord for revelation concerning what the places you dream about mean to you.

B: Scenes

Write down the scenes in the dream. Once again you might find yourself in a scene that is familiar to you.

Restaurants can speak of being fed while bathrooms can speak of being exposed or a season of cleansing in your life. Bedrooms speak of intimacy and privacy. You would need to identify what the scene means to you and if you sensed a positive or negative feeling towards that scene in your dream.

C: Identifying the Characters

Take each character in the dream and identify what part of you they represent if the dream is internal.

Some Hints:

- If they were people you know, then write down your relationship with them or what they mean to you.
- If they were people you did not know, note what your impressions were of them in your dream.
- If they are relatives, note how close you are to them. If a spouse, then your relationship with your spouse will determine the symbol. It could be positive or negative. Learn to identify this one because it will recur.

Often a spouse can speak of your recreated spirit in Christ. If you had a really good relationship with your earthly father, he could speak of the Lord in your dreams. If you have a bad relationship with a certain person, it is possible that they represent your flesh or sinful nature in your dreams.

If you often find yourself dreaming of a man or woman that you do not know, but yet they seem familiar to you, they could represent your masculine and feminine nature.

The masculine often represents left-brained, intellectual thinking, while the feminine represents the prophetic, right-brained emphasis.

If there is a person in your life who is strong and who you look up to, they could speak of the Holy Spirit and His protection.

The Relationship Is Vital to Interpretation

Your relationship with the person in your dream, in real life is vital in identifying what they represent.

Your sub-conscious mind will use your emotions and thoughts to convey the appropriate message to you clearly.

Often your sub-conscious will use people that represent something in your life. Perhaps the music leader in your church could represent your musical gifts. If you are a prophet, you might be at constant loggerheads with your pastor. In that case he could speak of the status quo church system in your dreams.

Often your children speak of your ministry or those things you have birthed in the spirit.

Dreaming about giving birth or being pregnant can speak of something you are about to birth in the spirit or have given birth to.

If you dream of babies dying it could be a warning dream that the thing the Lord has given you is dying.

D: Objects

- Note if the object means anything special to you.
- Does the object convey a negative or positive impression to you?

Often if you keep dreaming of coffins it could mean the Lord is letting you know that something in your flesh needs to die or perhaps has already died and you need to let it go.

This dream is very common amongst those in the ministry offices that are called to die to the flesh so that the spirit can dominate.

Dreaming of dead bodies is not always an attack from the enemy but a message from the Lord to just let die, that which is corrupt and rotten!

A wedding ring can speak of a covenant and a wedding dress of your union with the Lord or those things you are "married" or "tied" to.

E: Vehicles

It is also common to see vehicles in your dreams as your ministry - those things that "drive" your ministry. Often you may dream that you are driving and you are encountering difficulty. The Lord could be saying that you need to give over the wheel to Him and to stop taking your ministry out of His hands.

Perhaps you will dream that a person who symbolizes the Lord is driving in which case it is a good interpretation, indicating that the Lord is in control and that you can sit back and relax for a while. Dreaming that your vehicle has broken down can speak of some kind of damage that you have faced in your ministry.

There are even those dreams in which you dream you get new keys and are given a new car! This speaks of promotion and the Lord could be confirming that He has given you a greater anointing to carry out the ministry He has given you.

Then there are those objects from the Word that are often displayed in our dreams. Gold objects speak of the Lord and His deity, while a clay pot may speak of us as His vessels ready for service.

Wine often speaks of the anointing, as does water and oil. Arrows or weapons piercing you can speak of the work of the enemy who is known for his darts of destruction. Then again wielding a sword speaks of carrying the authority of the Lord and using it as a weapon against the enemy.

If you are not sure on the interpretation of an object take a look through the Word. It is rich with revelation and symbols. The Lord has been speaking in dark sayings and symbols to His prophets since the beginning of the world and you are certain to find the answer to your revelation right in the Scriptures!

F: Creatures/Animals

- Animals and insects - can refer to demonic powers but it depends also on how you view them.
- Plants and trees - can refer to growth, or barrenness if they are in bad condition.

- Babies or children - things that have been birthed or are still immature.

Snakes, spiders and black creatures in your dreams, very often speak of the work of the enemy and his attacks.

A lion can speak of the strength of the Lord. A lamb speaks of innocence and salvation. If you dream of your pet, you would need to identify what that pet means to you. Often pets are substitutes for children in which case they would represent a positive aspect of you.

G: Colors and Senses

- Things that were said or that you heard.
- Things you felt, tasted, smelled.

Often the color red can speak of the Lord's blood. Blue is a heavenly color, while black does not have a good connotation, being likened to the nature of the enemy. Gold often speaks of the Lord and His majesty, while silver speaks of humanity and redemption in the Scriptures. It is also used when referring to finance.

White can speak of purity and green of fertility. Once again you would need to identify what they mean to you as an individual and what they represent in the Word.

STEP 4: Get Revelation!

Once you have made your list and identified what each symbol represents, put the dream aside and summarize now what you have received from the Holy Spirit.

Write this final summary as a journal and so let it flow not from your intellectual thinking, but by using the internal anointing the Lord has given you for revelation.

Do not use the same formula on every dream you interpret. Allow the Holy Spirit to speak to you and give you additional visions and revelations to back up what you feel the dream means.

Here is where you are going to give the person (or yourself) the direction and answers you are looking for. It is not good enough to just give an interpretation without following it up with the Word of God to encourage, exhort and promote faith, hope and love.

If a warning is being indicated then give the warning and with it Scripture and direction on how to be victorious in that particular situation. If the dream is internal then guide the person who had the dream through a better understanding of what is going on inside themselves and how to move on from where they are.

If the dream is an internal prophetic one, then prepare the subject for what lies ahead and how to prepare for the work the Lord is about to do in their lives.

If the dream is external, receive revelation from the Spirit and Word on what to do with the revelation. In other words, find out if it needs to be spoken forth as a decree, kept for a later time, to be travailed over in intercession, or to be shared with a group that you might intercede in unity with.

In Conclusion

James 5 verse 1 says that if any man lacks wisdom all he needs to do is ask of the Lord and it will be given to him. So ask and pray for wisdom. Daniel was known for the wisdom the Lord gave him with dreams and so with the indwelling of the Holy Spirit we have that wisdom within us for every revelation and dream.

Receive that wisdom by faith and see the Lord open your eyes to a whole new realm of interpretation. As you allow yourself to be His vessel, He will open the way for you to use that gift and to bless the body of Christ with it.

Hearing God
Through Visions

Chapter 04 – Hearing God Through Visions

Whenever I stand up to minister, I preach using the visions that the Lord gives me. I see pictures and I just explain them to you. It is very simple. The key is to just be at peace. If you have pushed enough Scripture down into your spirit, it is very easy for those pictures to come back up.

When you want to receive a vision from the Lord, guess which pictures will come to your mind first?

Answer: The ones you have put down into your spirit.

If you do not put anything down, the Lord will still use you to minister with visions, but it is better if you have a spirit full of the Word - that way He has something to work with. He has lots of good stuff to give back to you when you need it.

However, if you are not pushing the Word down in the first place, you will struggle to receive visions because you have not put the pictures there.

Or on the other extreme, the pictures that come up will be filled with ideas from the world or whatever else you have been feeding your spirit with.

If you are spiritually dry though and have not fed on the Word, flowing in visions will dry up. This is especially true for people that have studied too much theology and doctrine.

Don't Be a Dry Cement Bag

These people are like dry cement bags. They have houses and houses of cement bags and then they try to flow in the spirit but cannot. Do you know why? It is because they have built their house out of cement bags, instead of combining the Word and Spirit together.

The problem is that they are so stuck in theology which does not have any pictures. It is all about verse "this" and verse "that". They give these long verses and nobody understands them. In fact, you have to spend hours trying to memorize and learn their technical jargon just to grasp what they are saying.

What pictures did you put into your spirit? You study the dry logos and then cannot understand why you are not receiving visions or flowing in the spirit. It is because all you have pushed down is dry stuff. No pictures at all.

If you want to start flowing in the spirit, you need to start by putting pictures from the Scriptures into your spirit.

Now, as you start to flow in the spirit, journaling comes quite naturally, because all you have to do is write down what you see. (I cover journaling in a later chapter).

What's a Vision?

> *2 Corinthians 12:1 It is not expedient for me doubtless to glory. I will come to visions and revelations of the Lord.*

In this passage above it is clear that Paul was used to receiving visions from the Lord, but this way of hearing from Him is not restricted to the apostle alone. In fact, every believer can hear the Lord through visions. As a prophet though you will function in this more than most.

I thrive on visions whether I am sharing this with you, preaching from the pulpit, playing a song, singing in the spirit, walking down the road, talking to the Lord... I am living in visions.

So what's a vision? Let me make it plain. A vision is simply a picture in your mind. What I love about visions is that they give you the next step along the road. The Word says that He is a light to our feet and a light to our path.

Visions are like the lamp, just there by your foot. Visions do not give you the full picture all at once.

You will find that when the Lord gives you revelation, He gives it to you a piece at a time. He doesn't offload the whole thing on you at once. It comes a piece at a time. You are going to experience that He will give you one little picture, and as you receive that and as you share that piece, you will receive more.

I want you to start experiencing visions in your private prayer times, in your times with the Lord whether you are reading, talking to the Lord or submitting the day to Him. I want you to be sensitive to the pictures that He puts into your mind.

This is the language of heaven. This is the language of the Lord. He speaks in pictures. Learn to identify them in every aspect of your life.

How Visions Work

Visions are the Lord using the sense of sight – sending you a picture from your spirit. That is why most visions you will receive will come from deep within.

The pictures and words you receive will come as impulses and deep impressions. They will be gentle and will flow as rivers of living water.

Vision Types

> **Mark 4:33** *And with many such **parables** he spoke the word to them, as they were able to hear [it].*

When Jesus walked the earth He spoke in parables and pictures to illustrate His point. And in all these years, He hasn't changed. He loves to give us pictures. Why? We remember pictures. Pictures stick with us.

It is hard to remember a prophetic word, but it is easy to remember an illustration. Let's be honest, you and I are both still thinking about the house that almost fell apart that I spoke about at the beginning.

The Lord will do the same. He will put pictures in your mind, and use visions to speak to you. This is something that you can develop more and more.

It is great to go on impressions, the audible voice and stuff like that, but without visions it's like being a blind man.

Visions are like taking a snap shot with the camera - it tells the story. You know, I could sit here and try to explain to you what a rose looks like or I could take a picture of it so you could see the colors for yourself.

What is going to be more effective? Well, it's the same in the spirit. You can understand the Word and get impressions from your spirit, but when you see visions in your spirit, it puts it all into place for you.

So visions are a very important way of being able to hear the voice of God. Do you flow in visions? If so, develop it! Fantastic! Let it become the most important thing to you.

If you are not there yet, then do not be discouraged, because it is quite likely that you are flowing in this way already without realizing it.

The Three Vision Categories

1st Category: Prophetic Visions

> **John 7:38** *He that believes in me, as the scripture has said, out of his inward parts will flow* ***rivers*** *of living* ***water***

This is by far the category that the Holy Spirit uses most to speak to His people. I used the passage above, because hearing God in this way feels very much like described here.

These visions flow out from deep within, like rivers of water. This is probably the most difficult concept to grasp for many people, even though it is the easiest to master.

In fact, the Lord Jesus is speaking to you all the time in impressions and visions – you just do not recognize this. This is a struggle I have seen with so many prophets that have come to us for training.

Having been used to hearing from the Lord externally, they wait for their visions to be suspended in front of them or for them to fall in a trance to say, "I received a vision from God!" Sure, God does speak in this way also, but it is not the primary method He uses.

Unfortunately, many have gone about seeking these experiences and have certainly found them... but not all can be accredited to the Holy Spirit!

Have you ever wondered why deception is running rampant amongst the prophetic ministry? It is the continuous "searching" that believers are doing for the open vision.

Rest assured that God is speaking to you right now in visions. It is the most articulate language of the spirit, because sight is our strongest sense.

He speaks today like He did to Apostle Paul when he saw a Macedonian inviting him to come and preach to them. The Macedonian was a symbol of the people that God was sending him to.

Now I cover interpreting symbols to your visions in my *Dreams and Visions* book, so I am not going to belabor the point here.

Rather I want to draw your attention to the fact that you are hearing God right now. Do you know those "impressions" you have been seeing when you pray? Those are visions!

However, when you are expecting to go into a trance or for the Lord to "slam" you with an open vision, you will miss the fact that you could be having a conversation with the Lord every moment of your day.

These visions are simple pictures that come from your spirit, leaving an impression on your mind. You might be journaling or praying with someone and you will get an "impression" of a river that is blocked. That is a vision!

When you "get it" that you have been seeing visions all along, a whole new world will open up to you. Then you can focus on that and expect it and you will discover that God has been talking to you all along.

Prophetic visions are pictorial impressions that come to your mind from your spirit.

2nd Category: Trance Visions

> *Acts 11:5 I was in the city of Joppa praying: and in a trance I saw a **vision**, A certain vessel descend, as it had been a great sheet, let down from heaven by four corners; and it came even to me:*

Our second category of visions is the kind that Peter had while waiting for lunch to be ready. This is a vision where your senses are suspended. You suddenly smell, feel or see things in the spirit that you are not feeling in the natural.

Your eyes are closed and it feels as if you are somewhere else. John G Lake certainly operated in this very strongly, which is no surprise because he was an evangelist. He would pray for someone from a long distance and see them being healed in the spirit, even though he was not there.

The scripture above is one of the very few instances where this type of vision is mentioned, which makes one think... When you consider the message of this vision I understand why the Lord gave Peter a trance instead of just a simple prophetic vision.

Consider that in this vision Peter even struggled with the Lord. He really did not want to hear this message! He tried to denounce it, but it was so strong, that he had to sit up and pay attention.

Had the Lord tried to give Peter this message as a prophetic vision, I can guess that he would have brushed it aside as his "imagination" and not thought about it further. However, God really had a point to make here.

He had to work through Peter's prejudice and open his eyes to an entirely new secret about the New Testament Church. Never once did it occur to Peter that salvation was also for the Gentiles... not until that vision that is!

So clearly God needed to make a point and I would daresay that those that function often in this vision type are ones where God is really trying to get His message across.

In a trance vision, the Lord suspends your senses, because He needs you to put your own ideas aside and listen to him.

This is what Eli found out when he decided to argue with the angel that told him that he would be the father of John the Baptist! The Lord made such a point, He struck Eli dumb!

So if you have flowed in this kind of vision, take note because the Lord had a strong message for you that you are meant to obey. If you do not flow in this way, then you can take a deep breath of relief. Perhaps you are ready to hear God and not "brush aside" His message so He does not need to suspend your senses!

3rd Category: Open Visions

> *Numbers 24:4 He has said, which heard the words of God, which saw the **vision** of the Almighty, falling [into a trance], but having his eyes **open**:*

You will notice that open visions are only mentioned very rarely and only in the Old Testament. There are a number of reasons for this. The first is that the Holy Spirit was not indwelling in the Old Testament.

When God spoke to man, He had to do so externally. He appeared when He willed and only for short periods of time. In the New Testament we can hear God any time we need to!

Just imagine, in the Old Testament they did not have the luxury of an internal "Urim and Thummim." They had to schlep all the way to the high priest to hear from God.

The same is true with visions – they had to wait for the Lord to come upon them to hear Him. Well, in this scripture used in this passage, it is quite an interesting occurrence. What makes it interesting is that Balaam was a false prophet!

Balaam

In fact, he had opened his mouth, ready to curse Israel and in the moment he opened his mouth to speak, God stepped in and took over. Instead of speaking that curse, as his eyes were open and he was looking over the tents of Israel, a completely different picture was superimposed over it.

In other words, his eyes were open, but what he saw was not the reality, but a picture God wanted him to see.

In an open vision a picture is superimposed over your natural senses. Your eyes see what God wants them to see – such as in the case of Balaam.

The Lord literally took Balaam over to make sure that His perfect will was spoken forth instead of the curse.

I think it stands to reason that if God has to take you over and shout at you so loudly… that you really are not terribly open to hearing His voice and have your own agenda.

I am not saying that God does not speak in this way today – He is God, He can do what He pleases! I am saying that in our New Testament era, He does not need to shout as He did in the past.

He does not need to wait for a moment to come upon us and bend us to His will. As His children and as His groom, He speaks to us from within. He has filled us with rivers of living water and He will flow out from within.

Colette Toach

Now it is quite possible that the Lord would use this kind of vision in an environment where a strong word needs to be spoken and the person He is speaking to needs to get it right down to the letter.

However, this is not normally the realm of the prophet and if you can flow more in prophetic visions, you will find your ministry leaping to the next level.

If Trance and Open Visions Stopped

If you flowed in trance and open visions and then they stopped, do not be concerned! The Lord is not suddenly ignoring you. In fact, I would daresay that you got the message and you are open to hear Him without Him having to shout.

I wish that I could say the same about good old Balaam though. He was so stubborn God made his donkey prophesy!

New Testament Difference

The indwelling of the Holy Spirit has changed everything. Where before only the select few could hear Him, the Scripture now says that:

> **Acts 2:17** And it will occur in the End Times, says God, that I will pour out from my Spirit onto every kind of person: and your sons and your daughters will prophesy, and your young people will see **visions**, and your seniors will have **dreams**:

The spirit of God is now poured out from us all! Every single one of us can hear from God!

So weigh your revelations carefully and vet them through your mentor or spiritual leader. Hopefully this has given you a good picture of what visions are and how to flow in them.

They are a powerful way to hear the Lord's voice and once you master this, the other 4 ways I am going to mention here will build upon that foundation.

Hearing God Through Tongues and Utterance

Chapter 05 – Hearing God Through Tongues and Utterance

> *1 Corinthians 14:18 I thank my God, I speak with **tongues** more than all of you*

I have had many opportunities in my life to learn different languages. In the country that I grew up in, there were eleven official languages. So depending on where you lived in the country you would learn that region's tribal language.

Unfortunately, we moved around a lot, so I never really got to learn any of these languages properly. Every six months we went from one place to the other. Just when I started to learn a bit of one language, we would move and I had to start all over again.

As a result, I must admit, I was left with some pretty bad thoughts on how to learn a language. It seemed really hard for me because I could never get the hang of it.

When I got a bit older and went into ministry and the Lord moved us to the opposite end of the world - I had to learn all over again. Now I was in a Spanish-speaking world and I had to learn some Spanish... At least enough to say, "Hey, where is the bathroom?"

And so I was faced again with having to learn new languages. Once I got over all my bad past experiences and fears, it actually became a lot of fun.

One thing that I think is clear for everyone starting for the first time, is that it is not always easy. What is exciting though is when you finally get it right.

I experienced this for the first time in Europe when I could finally speak a bit of German. I went to Germany where I had my first full conversation with a stranger that I met there.

Okay, sure... I was asking him about the chicken and how much it cost ... but the point was, I could ask it in his native tongue. Even better – he actually understood me! It was so exciting! It lit such a fire in me that I could communicate to a whole new world of people.

Suddenly languages became a very exciting thing.

Flowing in Tongues

Now when it comes to the world of the spirit there is also a language that we have to learn and it is called speaking in tongues. I tell you what is exciting about speaking in tongues - you don't have to go through all that tough learning. You don't have to get all the books and audio-visuals.

It is a gift that we receive in the spirit, but just like I had to learn to speak German to be able to communicate with a

German speaking person it is the same with the spirit. If you are going to understand the realm of the spirit and the messages of the spirit, you need to speak its language and that language is the gift of tongues.

I tell you, this is a very special gift because it is not just about speaking the right things, but it has the power to tap into your spirit and to do things in your spiritual life that you probably haven't even begun to understand.

I think that especially with people like me that grew up in a charismatic, Pentecostal environment, speaking in tongues was the first thing you did. From when I just knew the Lord, I just knew about speaking in tongues.

It becomes so commonplace that you really lose the power that it has to transform your life.

In my opinion this is one of the most important gifts that you need to possess. It is the starting point of all the other gifts of the Spirit.

Now I am not going to get into doctrinal controversy here and say that you are not saved if you cannot speak in tongues. I don't think that we need to take it and make a God out of it separately from the Lord Jesus. Simply put - without it you have a serious lack in your spiritual life.

It is like lacking the power of the atom bomb and just trying to use a little peashooter against the enemy.

Speaking in tongues gives you the power that you need to tap into the realm of the spirit. Not only that, it gives you the power to release what you have received from the Lord in the spirit.

Purpose for Speaking in Tongues

As you start speaking in tongues, you get rid of all the junk you put there and you start to feed your own spirit. Once you have fed your own spirit you will have enough anointing to pour out to everyone else around you.

You really need to take that time. It is like a chef that spends all his time cooking and preparing food. There comes a time when he has to sit down and eat himself.

There has to come a time in your spiritual walk when you stop and feed your own spirit so that you can feed others.

There is a danger if you minister to others very often, If you don't take time to charge up, you carry on doing what you have always done and then your "revelations" are going to start coming from your mind.

You will no longer feel the anointing - this is probably the biggest problem of all. You start to lack the anointing and it is because you haven't taken the time to tap into your spirit.

I hope I am really challenging you back to the basics. What is really the purpose for speaking in tongues?

1. Builds Your Spirit Up

Firstly, speaking in tongues builds up your own spirit and I have just covered that.

I had a couple of bodybuilders in my family on my mother's side. In fact, my grandfather was a keen weight training fanatic right into his older years.

He and my uncles were these big strong guys with bulging muscles. When we went on vacation together or he stayed at our house during holidays, instead of sleeping in like the rest of us, he was usually up at six or seven in the morning, in the gym pumping weights.

I thought to myself, "That's the craziest thing. You are supposed to be taking a break. You are supposed to be chilling out." And there he was... at the gym.

But you know... that's why he looked the way he did, because he was always building up his muscles. If ever he had to stop and not do it anymore, he would lose those muscles, that power and strength.

Tap Into Your Inner Bodybuilder!

Well, it is the same in the spirit. What you need to ask yourself is, "Is there a spiritual body builder inside of me, or a weedy little nerd?"

Well, that depends on how much you have been building your spirit up. Don't think that because a year ago you were this big muscular tough guy in the spirit that you are there now.

Unless you maintain it on a regular basis, you are going to lose that edge. Just like in the natural, you have to keep going to the gym and putting the effort in. When you put the effort in, you reap the fruits of it.

Do you want a nice, strong, muscular spirit? Then you need to continue speaking in tongues and make it part of your daily life. Then you can be that big spiritual bodybuilder that is strong and muscular and ready to take on anything that comes your way.

2. Cleanses Your Spirit

One of the most exciting things about tongues and its most practical uses is that it cleans out your spirit fast!

This is a powerful principle that is easily forgotten. We get so busy striving and trying to please the Lord that you get distracted. You forget that there is a very simple way to get back into His presence and to bring your spirit in line.

You can get spiritually fit again, by just taking time to speak in tongues.

Have you been distracted? Perhaps you have had a tough week and all hell has broken loose against you. Speaking in tongues gives you the life you need.

Perhaps you are frustrated and you are battling to hear the Lord's voice. You think to yourself, "Was that the Lord or was this my imagination again?"

Speaking in tongues brings your spirit to life. It separates the dross from the gold. It comes with a dividing line. It separates the spirit from the flesh like oil and water.

Sometimes things can look a little bit mixed up and you don't know what's the flesh and what's the spirit because it is all so confused. Speaking in tongues brings that clear division.

Speaking in tongues is like drilling through rock to sink a pipe into an underground stream for the purpose of setting up a windmill. Once the windmill is all set up, all you need is for the wind to blow and the living water springs up from the ground.

Getting to that point though takes a bit of effort. The best way to make sure you have God's fresh water on tap is by speaking in tongues for long periods of time.

Setting up Your Windmill

Now perhaps your pipe has gotten a little bit clogged along the line. It got a bit jammed up with stress, the fight that you had with your spouse, the struggles you are having at work and the conflicts you are having at church. Through it all, you get plugged up and contaminated.

At first you don't realize it, but slowly you notice that you have lost "the edge" when you minister. Don't think that your spirit is always just free because you are in ministry all the time.

Sometimes you can get so hung up on doing the work of the ministry and on pouring out that you can get clogged up and dull in your spirit because you have forgotten to tap into the life source.

If you have been the kind of person that has been running around and ministering to others and pouring out of the portion that you have, the chances are that after a while you are going to start feeling a little bit dry.

You will start pouring out from your intellect and you will begin to rely on what you know in your head. You will stop giving people the life force of the spirit that is inside of you and swap it out for a bunch of rotten manna.

Speaking in tongues changes all of that. It allows you to firstly get your mind out of the way, because you are not sitting concentrating on all the cares and problems, and coming up with logical solutions. Then it starts to tap into the stream of life inside of you.

Speaking in tongues is one of the best ways to tap into that anointing and to make sure, that what you speak comes gushing out with fresh (spiritual) water.

Utterance

> *1 Corinthians 14:5* *I want you all to speak with tongues, but I would prefer it if you prophesied: for he that prophesies is greater than he that speaks with tongues, unless he interprets, that the church might be built up.*

Now there comes a time though when you can't always speak in tongues all the time. There comes a time when you have to speak English.

It is great when a bunch of believers get together and you carry on in tongues for hours. In fact, you can all have a wonderful time and share in the presence of the Lord.

Even Apostle Paul said in the passage above, "Guys, if you are in a public meeting, if you are going to speak in tongues, you have to speak out the utterance. You have to speak it in the native tongue, so that everybody there can be edified and the Lord can reveal what is in their hearts."

If you have the opportunity in a local church, it is a fantastic opportunity. If you are new to utterance and interpretation though, then the best way for you to "get into the flow" is to do so in your prayer closet!

In fact, this is the way I learned to interpret my own tongues – I did so in the privacy of my prayer closet where the only ones to bare the brunt of my fumbling and mistakes was the pile of laundry I had yet to pack away.

The Difference Between Utterance and Interpretation

Now before I speak more on how to flow in utterance, let me interrupt myself here quickly and clarify the difference between utterance and interpretation. The secret lies in the following passage:

> *1 Corinthians 14:27 If any person speaks in an [unknown] tongue, [let it be] through two, or at the most [through] three [utterances], and in turn; and let one [person] interpret.*

To put it plainly – an utterance is a flow of inspired tongues that comes from your spirit. Interpretation is the interpretation of those tongues in your native language.

Perhaps you have seen this in effect in a meeting. I sure grew up with it all my life. Someone would stand up during worship and belt out a confident string of inspired tongues. Followed by that was a strong silence as everyone wondered, "Who will bring the interpretation?"

Then followed by that, the natural sigh of relief as the "usual guy" stood up and interpreted. The sigh of relief stemming from, "Whew! I am glad the guy speaking out that utterance did not miss it, mixed with – whew I am glad that God did not call on me to bring the interpretation!"

Learning to Flow in Utterance and Interpretation

The key though with all of this, is to do it in your private prayer time first. Don't feel pressured that you have to be a big hotshot out there and be like everybody else and do your message out there.

You know, you can practice this in your quiet time with the Lord and learn to develop this ability. Prophesy over yourself. Prophesy over your children. Speak in tongues and pray for people you know well. Develop it. Take your time. Learn to become familiar with this language of the spirit.

When I first started learning how to speak a different language I wasn't so arrogant that I went out immediately to find a German speaking person and tried to hold a conversation with the whole two German words I knew.

Some people are that arrogant and they are annoying. I didn't want to be annoying. I wanted to make sure I could at least speak a sentence that they could understand.

Do the same with the spirit. Learn a bit. Take time to get to know the realm of the spirit. Take your time to get to know the voice of the Lord.

Then when you step out you are going to do it with confidence. You are going to have good experiences, not bad experiences that are going to leave you feeling discouraged.

Sing in Tongues

A fantastic way to learn to interpret your tongues is to praise and worship in tongues during your private times with God.

If you want to take your spiritual life to a whole new level try interpreting your tongues by singing on your guitar, on your piano or while you are driving your kids to school (if they can bear it).

Take the time to interpret your tongues while you are singing. Sing it out. It is a fantastic first step to learning how to prophesy in song and it is something that I learned to do a very long time ago.

I can't actually remember when it was because it became such a part of my life and ministry.

Every time you go into worship, every time you lead the worship, you can guarantee that there is going to be something new - a new song and that the Lord is going to give you new wisdom. So give that a try and you will be amazed at the sudden increase of anointing.

There is something about music. When you combine tongues, music and interpretation there is such power there. So give this a try in your next prayer time and see what happens. Soon you will be raving about it just as much as I am.

Tongues, utterance and interpretation are a powerful way to hear God's voice and the more time you spend in the Word and in the Spirit, the more you can expect to hear God in this way.

Once you are familiar with this, flowing in prophecy and moving onto journaling is a natural progression. Although I do not teach you how to hear the voice of God through prophecy in this book, I do cover it in some detail in the Prophetic Functions book.

How to Hear God Through Journaling

Chapter 06 – How to Hear God Through Journaling

> *1 Chronicles 28:19 All [this, said David], the LORD [Yahweh] made me understand in writing by [his] hand upon me, [even] all the works of this pattern*

One of the first things that I taught my children when they were old enough was how to have a conversation. Now, you would think that this is something natural to us humans, but actually I discovered that it wasn't.

A child is not born knowing how to have a good conversation with somebody. In fact, usually kids are very one-sided in their conversation. They are more like, "Look at me" and they talk about everything they did.

And so especially being in active ministry and being involved with a lot of people, I had to teach them the social skill of having a conversation. As a mother I taught them to say things like, "How are you?"

"You look lovely today!"

"How many children do you have?"

I realized that it really was an art. I only saw the fruit of this when they were a little older and I met somebody who had met the kids before me.

The lady said, "I was so amazed. Your kids showed an interest in the kind of person I was. I never met children like that before. They came into my home and said, 'Wow, you've got such a lovely home. How long have you lived here?'"

She said, "They asked questions that children just never ask and it was such a pleasure just to have a conversation with them."

It made me quite the proud mom!

The Art of Journaling

You know, these skills are developed - they are not something that we are born with. We learn how to develop conversation and as we come to the subject of journaling, it is very much the same.

A good definition of journaling is this – a written conversation with the Lord.

It is a written dialog between you and the Lord where you approach Him with your thoughts and ideas and write back what He tells you.

He might speak to you in visions or you might hear a still small voice. It is much like operating in utterance or prophecy – you simply write down what you would ordinarily say out loud.

What It Looks Like

Journaling looks like this,

"Lord, I am having another bad day. I did not get any sleep last night because the kids kept me up and I still have not done my laundry. I do not feel like getting out of bed today, Lord."

The Secret to Hearing

Then you give the Lord a chance to talk. That is one of the secrets to hearing His voice. You have to be real with Him. Say it like it is. Come to Him as you are. As you come and journal and write down all your pitiful woes, how sad you are and whatever else, then you quiet your spirit.

Now, a picture will come to you, a memory will come to you or a scripture will come to mind, and all you need to do is start writing it down. The secret in writing it down is to not write in third person, but to write it as if it is coming directly from the Lord.

So, after I have written my part, I close my eyes and say, "Okay Lord, what do you have to tell me?" Then I see a picture of a river meandering through an open field that is lush, green and beautiful. How do I vocalize that?

It would look a little like this,

"It is time to come into my rest, my child. Come and sit by the water and rest in the river because you have been in so much chaos. It is time to put your problems aside and to just come into my presence and sit by the stream for a little while."

You are journaling! It takes a little bit of practice and for the first while, it will probably be straight from your mind. Relax. It is okay. It is not like you have committed the unpardonable sin by hearing from your mind and not from God.

It Is OK to Mess Up

It does not have to be perfect from the start. Have you ever heard a child learning to speak? My son, Michael, couldn't say "Denise" when he was three years old. He said, "Neese" instead. He could not speak full sentences. He said, "I come with" and "hot tea, please" or more like "hot tea, pwease."

He could not pronounce the letter "l" correctly at first, but after a while, he got the words right. When he first started going "ma ma" or "da da", I did not say, "Would you please say, mother, father, sister, brother and can I hear you quote the books of the Bible please?"

No, give the guy a break. He is just learning to speak! He will get there in time. Just like a baby needs time to learn to speak, we need time to learn to hear His voice correctly. Yes, some of what you write down will be your thoughts and ideas.

However, the more you do it, the better you will get. Then you will look over older journals and see the parts that were God and the parts that were you. The more you get used to hearing His voice, the more you will recognize where you are getting off track.

It is a process. It is a relationship. Even in marriage relationships, it takes a while to understand what the other person is "really" saying. It takes time to get to know one another. It is the same with the Lord.

Upbringing Conditions You

Unfortunately, there are a lot of preconceived ideas that you have from growing up in the Church. Most of the skills we have in getting along with people come from the home.

Depending on the kind of relationship you had with your parents and siblings will determine how well you can have a conversation.

So you come to the Lord, ready to share your heart and hear His voice and find yourself in a bind.

The problem is that you have so many ideas in your mind about how you should be approaching God and how you should be talking to Him that it starts to hinder your ability to journal.

What is journaling? Simply put it is a method of conversation via writing where you present your thoughts to the Lord and then you write down His answer.

Now learning how to journal is quite simple and it is a subject that I have already taught on extensively, so I am not going to re-hash that here. Rather I am going to assume that you know what journaling is and that you have already attempted it.

If you want to get more instruction on how to journal please read, The Way of Dreams and Visions, Practical Prophetic Ministry or Called to the Ministry.

Do's and Don'ts of Journaling

So in this chapter I just want to take a very quick look at the do's and don'ts for journaling. They are very practical so I really want you to pick up pen and paper or underline them in the book.

You know what should be done, but why be satisfied with what you have? There is always place to go deeper!

1. Listen

Take time to hear what God has to say. You might be thinking, "That's a no brainer - it is journaling after all!" but you would be surprised how many people are so busy talking to the Lord about their problems that they never stop to hear what He has to say.

Remember how I shared how I taught my children to ask questions and to listen to other people? That is such a vital part of journaling. Listen to what He wants to say. Don't get too self-absorbed.

It could be that the Lord wants to talk about something completely different. He wants to answer your question in a way you do not expect. I have experienced this many times in my own journals.

Listen to what God has to say. Really listen. Don't get so wrapped up in your ideas that you do not listen and He is literally shouting to you through the journal, but you keep trying to pull Him back to your point. Don't do it!

2. Make Your Request Clear

The next point is: Make your request clear. When you come to the Lord come with a clear idea of what you are journaling for. This helps to give you a tremendous direction for your journal.

If you just want to hear His voice then say "Lord, what do you have to say to me today? What is your direction for me today?"

Come with an idea of what you are going to say because it is a conversation. Say to the Lord, "Lord, this is my need and care" or "Hey, how are you doing? I just want to hear what you have to say."

By doing this, it gives you a clear track to run on – a direction for your journal. It is always nice when having a conversation with someone to "get it rolling." Then it can develop from there.

3. Be Real and Honest

When I am with a good friend, I don't say, "It would please me to have you accompany me to the nearest coffee shop, so that we might share a tasty beverage. Would you extend me the grace by accepting my eager invitation?"

My friends would look at me pretty strangely if I spoke like that! So it stands to reason that I don't talk in theatrical language and religious speech.

I just say, "Hey, how is it going? You want to come around for a cup of coffee?"

Well, Jesus is your best friend and you should be real and honest with Him, more so than you can be with any other person in this world.

There is no such thing as having to approach the Lord in a formatted, formal way.

Yes, by all means, have a healthy fear of the Father. It is important to have reverence, because He is God.

However, the kind of relationship that I am talking about here is an intimate relationship with the Lord Jesus.

The exciting thing is, when you are real and honest with Him, He is very real and honest back.

Are you looking for a straight answer to something? Then ask Him a straight question. Don't word your question in a way that sounds nicer than the reality - because He knows what's in your heart anyway!

Say it like it is. Say it how you feel it. Say what you are really thinking. Spit it out.

If you feel embarrassed about how it really is, delete the journal afterwards, okay? (If that makes you feel any better.)

This is a very good starting point to make your journals come alive and making the Lord feel more real. You get in touch with Him and you will start to hear some honest answers back.

4. Do not Paste in Tons of Scriptures

Under no circumstance should you paste in hundreds of scriptures. What's the point?

That is like having a conversation with a friend where you are trying to back up every statement you make with a scripture.

I hate to break it to you, but the Lord already knows what He said in the Word. He is the one that originated it. He doesn't need to quote it back at Himself.

I see this so often with the prophets. They are journaling and then they paste the scripture reference there just to back up what the Lord said.

In fact, the speech of the Word should be natural.

The Language of God

You will find that as the Lord speaks to you in your journals He is going to say things like, "My child, I have called you to be the head and not the tail, above and not beneath."

He does not give the disclaimer though, "Please go to Deuteronomy 28:44..." He doesn't do it because He knows where it's found. He spoke it. He originated it. He doesn't need to repeat it and He doesn't need to back Himself up.

Try to get away from it and I will tell you why. If you get into the "I have to go look up all the scriptures" mode, you cut the flow of your spirit and you get into your mind. That is when you start walking a delicate line that can even lead to deception.

By taking your mind off what God is saying and over analyzing it, you give the enemy the opening he needs to get his ideas in there.

If you are unsure about the content of your journal, then journal first and afterwards look up the scriptures.

5. Do Not Use High Spiritual Language

From what I have seen over the years I got the idea that many believers think that the Lord speaks in King James English.

Here is a newsflash... He doesn't! In fact, you will find that when Jesus walked the earth, He was rather ordinary. So much so that the Pharisees needed Judas to identify Him.

He was ordinary looking and ordinary in the language of the day He used.

Of course, the authority with which He spoke was something else altogether! There was surely nothing very ordinary with the power that those words were spoken with!

He spoke in such a way that the uneducated beggars understood Him. Prostitutes understood Him..

When He went to Nicodemus He had to say, "For somebody that is so educated, you are pretty stupid." He was talking so plainly that Nicodemus in his high spiritual understanding could not understand the plainness and the simplicity of His message.

He Talks My Language!

When you come into an intimate relationship with Jesus you will realize that He talks your language. He speaks like you speak.

If you speak French, He speaks French. If you speak English, He speaks English. He speaks to you in a way that you will understand Him.

The Lord doesn't speak in high-toned spiritual language all the time and He certainly does not speak in King James English. He speaks a language that you can understand. He speaks in pictures, types and shadows.

6. Do not Use Jargon and Spiritual Buzzwords

I realize that there are so many "Christian buzzwords" floating around in the Church. There are things that we have grown up with through the years, things that we have received from other ministries.

And so you just take them. You just say, "Oh, okay, I just take that. That's how it is." You don't stop to look in the Scriptures for yourself. These buzzwords end up becoming a doctrine in themselves because no one took the time to look them up.

So watch out for these little terms, especially those common terms that are out there that are not based on the Word.

Now you do not need to get paranoid - sure, there are some good ones that are based on the Word and the Lord will use them to illustrate His point. He will talk about named principles that you have studied to make a point.

Where Did It Originate?

That is just one of my little personal things and you can either take it with a pinch of salt or you could really take it as a challenge and say, "Yes, that's a good point. Why do I always say that? Where did I get that buzzword from?"

Perhaps you have a few ideas that come to your mind, but there are a few that I hear often.

"New level, new devil."

"Name it and claim it brother!"

"If it's His will, it's His bill!"

"Too blessed to be stressed"

"God is good all the time. All the time, God is good!"

If you want to journal like you never have before and come into an intimate relationship with the Lord, you need to cut through all the rubbish.

You will need to cut through the religious mindsets. Cut out the fancy language and misconceptions and you will find your relationship with the Lord becoming real, alive and evolving into something wonderful.

Here is a tip to help identify a buzzword – would you use that in a normal conversation? Remember, I was sharing how conversation is an art.

Final Challenge

So what are you going to do? Are you going to take up the challenge or are you going to say, "No, my journals are great. I have got it all together. I think it is pretty perfect."

Is it? Have you developed the art of conversation with the Lord to the point where you are so comfortable with talking to Him and with hearing what He has to say?

Are your journals still in point form, or do they look like a conversation? They should look as if somebody took the conversation and transcribed it.

It takes time to get it right, but I know that as you apply yourself, that you will soon come to the place where Jesus and you are talking face-to-face!

Hearing God Through the Audible and Still Small Voice

Chapter 07 – Hearing God Through the Audible and Still Small Voice

The Audible Voice

> *Acts 22:7 And I fell to the ground, and heard a voice saying to me, saul, saul, why persecute you me?*

Then you can hear the Lord through the audible voice. This is not as common, but it is certainly the way that Moses must have heard the Lord. You can hear Him audibly.

When somebody can only hear the audible voice though and doesn't flow in any of the other ways of hearing the Lord, I question it.

I question it a lot because if they can only hear the audible voice, but don't receive visions, can't journal, can't hear the Lord for themselves personally, then I begin to wonder.

I wonder what the voice is that they are hearing. Is it really the voice of the Lord? If the Lord has to shout all the time, you either do not know how to listen or the voice you are hearing is not of God and is in fact drowning out the still small voice from within.

God is talking 24 hours a day, you just need to listen. When I journal, worship or speak in tongues, I get visions, an Urim or Thummim. The moment I get into His presence, the revelation flows automatically.

So if somebody can only hear an audible voice and doesn't know how to journal or hear the Lord in any other way I am very suspicious and I want to test that spirit.

So if you have had that and can only hear Him through an audible voice, then something is wrong and I would question the voice you are hearing. I would get somebody to judge the spirit of it.

This would fall into the same category as an open vision. Yes, God is well able to speak in this way and He chooses to at times. However, it is not the only way that He speaks to His people.

You cannot tell the Church that the only way that they can hear God for themselves is to wait for an audible voice to come from the sky.

I have found that hearing God's audible voice has happened often to those who needed a clear confirmation of their salvation. It likely happened when they got born again or was even the purpose of them being saved. A good example of this of course is Apostle Paul on his way to Damascus.

The Lord had to stop him dead in his tracks. Accompanied with that voice was a blinding light and a back-hander, knocking him to the ground!

Fortunately for us all, Paul was pretty quick to get the message and the Lord did not have to resort to such extreme measures again to get through to him!

How to Hear the Voice of God

After that he knew with the spirit.

The Still Small Voice

> *1 Corinthians 3:16* Do you not know that you are the temple of God, and [that] the spirit of God dwells in you?

From the time we are born again, the Holy Spirit comes to dwell within us. The still small voice is by far one of the most common ways to hear Him.

In fact, it is likely you have heard this voice often, but have just not recognized it. So often we look for the loud voice, not realizing that Jesus is a gentleman.

That is certainly what Elijah experienced when he was running away from Jezebel in 1 Kings 19:12. He expected to hear the Lord in the earthquake, but instead heard Him in the gentle breeze.

This was a beautiful picture of what the Lord had in mind for us all along. As believers, we have the Holy Spirit within and that breeze is always blowing. You will hear it during times when you are crying out for an answer or when it is time to take a new direction.

How Do You Know if It's God?

When I am feeling weary, He lifts my arms from behind and says, "Push on through. You can do it."

The inner voice is the Lord speaking to you from your own spirit. In fact, it is a lot like receiving a vision, only it is words that are formed in your mind instead of a picture.

It Will Sound Like You

So how do you know if you are making things up or if it is really the Lord? The first time I was aware of this voice, I was sure I was making things up. It happened to me when I met Craig for the first time.

We were working as waiters in a popular restaurant and we bumped into one another during our work shift. As we met, I heard a voice in my spirit say, "Be careful how you handle this meeting, because this could be your future husband."

I thought I was "hearing things." Well, the Lord knew that I needed a little help because the road I was determined to walk at that time had me going in a very different direction to the way God wanted me to go!

When you first start paying attention to that inner voice, it starts off with the feeling, of "yes", "no", or "maybe". Then as you develop it more and practice His presence more, you will hear a very soft thought.

It will be a thought that sounds like you, but is coming from your spirit.

It will be a thought that says, "I love you."

"I would prefer it if you did not do that."

"I do not think this is a good idea."

"I really think you should go for that." You may not even be able to vocalize it word for word at the beginning.

It Will Be Gentle

It will be just an array of thoughts, but not pushy thoughts. It will be a gentle thought. Go through the other six ways of hearing His voice before you do this one.

The enemy will try to put pushy thoughts in your mind. You will need to know the Lord's voice well before listening this way.

You have probably had this already, especially in crisis situations where something happened and it is a really tough or dangerous situation. Suddenly, you get this thought that everything is going to be okay.

It does not even make sense because in the natural, everything is falling apart. The bills are due, the finances are not coming in, but you get this thought in your mind that everything will be okay and the rent will be paid.

You think, "Where did that thought come from?"

Very often when you are in these situations, thoughts will come to you. When you start realizing that those thoughts are the voice of the Lord and you link them to the Urim and Thummim you have been feeling and to the Word you have been pushing down, guess what happens?

Pictures start to build. You realize that God has been trying to tell you something all along. That is the wonderful thing about hearing the Lord's voice.

He does not only speak one way. He does not give you a prophetic word and that is it.

He will speak through the Urim and Thummim, visions and also in your journal.

Practicing His Presence Project

It will take time to really get to know Him. From there, you will start hearing the still, small voice. This takes a little longer to develop, but the best way to develop it is to practice His presence.

It is a very simple project. Everywhere you go, realize that Jesus is there with you. So as I am standing up to preach, I am imagining the Lord right there with me. He gives me notes every now and again. He gives me a squeeze on the shoulder every now and again and says, "You are doing great. Hang in there."

When I am feeling weary, He lifts my arms from behind and says, "Push on through. You can do it."

He says, "Hey, did you think about this?" I see Him right there and I sense His presence there with me.

Then we finish up and go to lunch and I imagine the Lord sitting there with me at the table. Then He says, "Watch this." I see the conversation turn. This person says something and sparks the next person off. Next thing you know, we are busy teaching.

Then we have to run to the store to get something and I imagine the Lord in the car with me. I say, "Okay Lord, what should we get today, chicken, sausage or what? Lord, do these pants make me look fat?"

Does that sound ridiculous? Well, I am practicing His presence. Wherever you go or whatever you do, take Him with you - even to the bathroom. Hey, it is nothing that the Lord has not already seen before.

Maybe you are watching the kids, going for a walk or answering phones in the office, it does not matter. You do not have to talk to Him all the time. People may think you are a little crazy (especially at work) but you can imagine Him there with you at all times.

It is not so far from reality because He is there. He is inside of you. The key is to bring Him to your mind and remember that He is there. When you start to do that, you cannot get away with doing what you usually do.

It Puts You in a Place to Hear His Voice

It brings conviction and puts you in a place to hear His voice. Since you are imagining Him there all the time, pictures will always be coming to your mind. You will feel impressions much stronger than before because He is right there and He is the one bringing them up.

While you are imagining Him there and say, "Lord, should I go here or not?" You will realize that you know the answer already. No - that is not something the Lord would do or... yes it is.

When the Lord is with you, it changes all your decisions. You are tuning into your spirit all the time. It is like flipping through radio channels and where you mostly heard static before, you will now hear a clear voice ring through.

When you practice His presence and learn to hear that still, small voice in your spirit, it is like finding the right frequency on the radio.

The Love Relationship

When you come to the place of walking in that relationship with the Lord Jesus, all the gifts and everything else will fall into line.

Paul gets us all fired up about the gifts of the Spirit in 1 Corinthians 12, only to end on the strangest low note. After ranting about how all of us have a place and how the Holy Spirit manifests the gifts through us, He ends by saying, "...but let me show you a better way."

Chapter 13 is the better way. It is the chapter on love.

As you come into this relationship with Jesus you will finally understand the passage that says:

> *1 Corinthians 13:8 [Agape] love never loses its efficiency: but if [there are] prophecies, they will come to an end; if [there are] tongues, they will cease; if [there is] knowledge, it will vanish away.*

That is the point of learning to hear God's voice. The purpose is not being able to prophesy or "get revelation". The point of it all is to come into the perfect knowledge of agape love.

It is only in the presence of Jesus that you will experience this love. It is only through hearing His voice for yourself that you will not only feel this love, but be able to pour it out as well.

Hearing God Through Circumstances

Chapter 08 – Hearing God Through Circumstances

You have learned how to hear God through the Word and the Spirit. As a result your cement is well mixed and you love flowing in the Spirit and hearing from the Word.

The question remains though – how do you know if these ideas of yours are from the Lord? Well, that is what you need this chapter for. The Lord will "seal" the revelation He has given to you by confirming through others!

It all starts out when you feel an impression in your spirit that you are called to something specific. You have been in the Word and it confirms what you think.

Then one day while you are in a meeting, the preacher preaches what has been in your heart the whole time. When this happens, the Lord is saying, "Hello!" The next thing you know, your circumstances change and an opportunity opens up and you stand there thinking, "I wonder if this is the will of God for my life?"

Of course "this" is the will of God for your life! He has been confirming His Word. The circumstances are just another confirmation of what He has been telling you all along.

Perhaps you get this great idea that you need to move across the country. Then all the doors close completely!

Everything stands against you. Somehow the Lord keeps opening up other doors. "Wake up!" The Lord is trying to tell you something.

"Oh, I am trying, but I am not getting any further revelation. I got a prophetic word or an idea that we must go in this direction, but the Lord is not speaking to me. He is not saying anything in my journals. I am not getting any confirmation." Then wait!

Word, Spirit, Circumstances – The Full Package

If the doors are not opening, maybe you are basing your revelation on the wrong things because God confirms His word to you. He speaks to you in the Word, to your spirit and then through circumstances. He does not reveal His will through "either - or" but through all of them at the same time.

That is how you know it is God's will. Isn't that great? You do not need to go around looking for signs. When you already have the impression in your spirit, the signs will come.

Say for example, you have been seeking the Lord to do something new in ministry. You have a fire in your heart that indicates that you need to get moving forward in your ministry. You feel this is really of the Lord.

Then you get into the Scriptures and read about when the Lord said to Moses, "Go and set my people free."

You think, "That burns in me. There is something in that word!" Then suddenly the Lord opens an opportunity for you to get involved in a ministry.

Then, you wonder if it is of God…? Of course it is of God. He has been talking to you and leading you up to this point. I am not saying you will not have warfare getting to this point, but that is a whole different story altogether.

God Uses Circumstances to Confirm

The point is, God uses circumstances to confirm the word that He has already given to you.

Now, there is a big caution in just using circumstances as a sign. The world does that all the time.

"Two birds flew over me. It is a sign that I must go in two directions at once."

"I saw two turtle doves and so the Lord is telling me there is a symbolism in the number two. He is saying we should do a double thing in this ministry."

Definitely not! The signs that God uses in circumstances should confirm what you have already received in the Word and in the Spirit. Then the circumstances come to confirm. Not the other way around.

You should not be saying, "Lord, what are you telling me here?" God should have already told you, if you were listening. The circumstance would just be a confirmation.

I get this all the time. I will be journaling and the Lord will say, "You need to concentrate more on this particular kind of counseling. You are very weak in this area and I want you to study." I start reading the Word and suddenly everywhere in the Scriptures, I start seeing the Lord bringing up the same point.

Next thing you know, we start getting phone calls and knocks on the door about people having these exact counseling needs. To me it is just a confirmation of what God has been saying all along.

I will ask the Lord when He wants us to have a seminar. Then I will start feeling in my spirit that it is time and I will say to my husband, "I feel we need to talk about this thing at the next seminar."

Then as I am in the Word the revelation starts to flow about what we are going to preach at the seminar. Suddenly someone on the team will contact me and say, "Mom, are we having a seminar any time soon because people keep calling in and asking when the next seminar will be?"

Bring the Pictures Together

That is how I hear the voice of God. You just need to bring all the pictures together, but you are waiting for this big voice to come out of the sky.

Confirmation Through Other People

In addition to confirming His will for you through circumstances, the Lord will also speak to you through people.

You might be having a conversation and someone will say something that will really annoy you, encourage you or somehow have an impact on you. Somehow it hits you and causes you to realize, "That was God's voice!"

You may not always like it and it may not always be pretty, but you cannot go left or right because you know that was God. If you have been pushing down the Word and sensing things in your spirit, you will recognize it.

You will go to a church meeting and the preacher will stand up and it will seem as if he is speaking directly to you.

"Oh well, that was just the preacher. "

No, that was the voice of God. He might have been using another man to speak, but you just heard the will of God for your life. What are you doing with it?

God uses so many different ways to get our attention. You just need to wake up and listen to it. I go through this with my kids. Sometimes I am going through stuff when templates and struggles are coming up all over the place.

Then my youngest daughter Ruby will walk up and just say something out of her childlike innocence and it feels like a sword right through my heart. I think, "That is the voice of God. I better listen to it. That is not a child speaking - that is God speaking to me."

Learn to identify that in others. Like I said, you may not always like it.

Identify His Voice

By now you should be able to sense when there is something powerful in the words others are speaking. They said of Jesus, "Never a man spoke as this man." Why? It was because of the power with which He was speaking. It was God speaking.

They could see the same power on the disciples when they spoke. God will use people around you. He will use children. He will use preachers from the pulpit. He will use prophets. He will use whoever is available for Him to use!

There will be times when someone is talking and you will think, "That is a bunch of bubble and froth", but then there will be other times when people will speak and you will say, "Oh yes, that is God. I feel that. There is something about what they just said that impacted my life."

Confirmation Through Teaching

Then of course, the Lord can lead you to books or websites, which is how many found us.

You suddenly find yourself on a website reading an article that feels as if you are not just reading something the author wrote, but something the Lord is saying directly to you. It strikes your heart. You just heard the voice of God and His will for your life.

Turn up the Volume

Let us put it all together. You have been hearing the will of God for your life all along. You just have not identified it. What you can do now is take the principles I have taught you and turn the volume up on the radio.

This way, His Word becomes a little clearer and you do not have to spend hours and hours in the Word before you start getting impressions in your spirit.

That is the wonderful thing about your spiritual walk - it is a progression. It will not happen all in one day. If you are not there yet, it does not matter. There is a goal and you can go as far as you need to or want to go.

Start where you are right now. Put pictures in your heart using the Word. Learn to listen to the impressions of your spirit during the day. Always practice His presence and keep Him close by.

Then be on the lookout for the articles you stumble across, the Christians you bump into or that preacher you are listening to. As you take the cement, water and bricks, everything will be put together and you will have a sturdy house built on a solid foundation.

The Purpose for Hearing His Voice

Have you noticed how easily people rub off on you? You make a new friend and before you know it, you are using phrases that they use. It is quite the thing in our ministry.

Because we are such an international ministry with team members from all over the world, we have rubbed off on each other so much that you can hear a whole variety of phrases around the dinner table.

Someone will ask for the salt in German, another will answer in Spanish as someone throws a typical American English slang.

You will notice that each church and community has a certain language of their own. You find your mindsets and likes being influenced by those around you. It is the way the Lord created us. He created us to connect with those around us.

Well, imagine for a moment that the Lord was the one doing most of the "rubbing off" on you…

How is this going to happen? The only way it can take place is when you put yourself in a place to hear His voice often. Soon you will find yourself using His catch phrases.

You will find His agape love rubbing off on you. Soon your walk with Him will not be about "gifts" and "revelations" but completely about relationship.

When you get to that point, then you have something to hand out to the body of Christ.

Experience Him in All 5 Senses!

So do not limit yourself! I have taught on different ways to hear His voice, but actually I have taught you on how to hear, see, feel, smell and taste His voice!

I have taught you to be sensitive to the messages that are coming from your spirit all of the time. Now imagine that you can combine them all.

Give it a try next time you are in His presence. Try to involve all your sense in hearing Him.

When you come to the Lord to receive direction – whether that is through prayer or journaling, be mindful of the following things:

1. What visions am I seeing? What pictures are coming up in my mind right now?
2. What sounds am I hearing right now? Am I hearing words or a specific sound?

3.   What do I feel inside of me right now? Urim? Thummim? Warning? Joy?
4.   What do I smell in the spirit? Am I aware of a fragrance?
5.   What do I taste in the spirit right now? Is there something "sweet in the air?"

Give it a try! By doing that, you allow yourself to experience the Lord in His fullness. It means that you are completely engaged with Him. It will not be long at all and the nature of the Lord will begin to show in you.

You see, that is what the fruit of the Spirit is all about. Have you ever wondered how to develop the fruit of the Spirit in your life? Well, this is the secret. Experience Jesus!

The more you are wrapped up in Him, the quicker you will pick up His nature and along with that every fruit of the Spirit. This is the natural progression of every believer.

However, before you can claim yourself the "expert on hearing God" it is a good idea to learn each way to hear His voice.

By this stage of your journey you will come to realize that it has become a lot more than just "hearing His voice" but about "becoming the image of Christ."

With that revelation, you are fast on your way to establishing the Church as a city on a hill – your life being the light that shines in the darkness.

About the Author

COLETTE TOACH

The Master Juggler... Most of the time anyway! Not only is Colette a talented writer with numerous books under her belt, but she is also a full time Mom of four children, awesome cook, powerfully anointed Christian minister/counsel, in your face trainer and an accomplished business woman. Oh yeah and she still gets to get her beauty sleep every now and again.

Having learnt everything in the trenches and rising through the ranks, Colette brings to the table an all-round understanding to any situation. Having been the follower and then thrust into leadership, she is able to see both sides of the coin and bring a fresh and new understanding. That is why her writings have become such an inspiration and blessing to many who have read her books.

That is why she can boldly challenge anyone, because her moto is "I expect nothing from you, I have not done myself!" her work is not just knowledge, but living knowledge.

From humble beginnings in Zimbabwe, Colette spent most of her Childhood and early teen years in South Africa. Having a personal experience and call to the ministry at age 13 and preaching her first sermon at age 14, it is no wonder her path would not be an easy one. Having faced poverty, divorce and rejection, it helped build a strong love for the Lord and compassion for His people. This foundation is what continues to bring forth powerful materials that reach a range of subject and have helped many to find the unanswered questions they always had; without them needing a bachelor's degree to understand it.

As the Co-founder of Apostolic Movement International, LLC based out of San Diego California USA, Colette and her husband along with their team, continue to produce materials, train and hold seminars to help bring change to the Body of Christ, making her a beautiful bride ready for her groom.

How does she do it? She will gladly tell you... By the Lord Jesus Grace alone and in her weakness!

For more about Colette, check out her blog site at: www.colette-toach.com

AMI Recommendations

If you enjoyed this book, we know you will also love the following books on the prophetic.

Called To The Ministry

By Colette Toach

God has put a purpose for your existence inside you. There is a driving force within you to accomplish something much greater than yourself and to fulfill the call of God on your life.

However… how do you know what that calling is?

Apostle Colette Toach takes you by the hand and helps you to realize the call of God that has been whispering to you all along.

It is the conviction of your calling that will fuel the fire to push through when times get rough. By teaching you how to KNOW His will for you and to hear clearly from Him, you will receive the conviction that will push you through the fire time and time again.

Learn how to experience His presence and you will no longer need not feel lost or insecure about the choices you will make. When you know how to get a rhema word from God, nothing can stop you from moving forward.

Then as you realize your calling, map out the training that is sure to come. Each fivefold ministry training is geared to shape you into a certain kind of vessel. Apostle Colette goes the extra mile and explains in detail which one(s) you will go through and what it is going to produce in you.

By the end of this book, you will know too much. So much so that you will be held accountable for fulfilling your call. There will be no more excuses as to why you cannot succeed. Apostle Colette releases an anointing in this book that will challenge, convict, motivate and launch you into your calling!

Table Of Contents

Chapters

1. What is Your Calling?
2. Knowing God's Will
3. Knowing God's Will Through the Spirit - the Water
4. Confirmation Through Circumstances - the Bricks
5. Experiencing God's Presence
6. Using the Word and Tongues (Bulldozing)
7. How You Feel the Anointing
8. Knowing Your Place in the Body
9. Remaining Body Ministries
10. Your Call to the Fivefold Ministry
11. Fivefold Ministry Training
12. Charting Your Course
13. The Prize of the Call
14. Your Final Destination

How to Hear the Voice of God

Fivefold Ministry School

http://www.fivefold-school.com

You Can be a Success in Ministry!

My passion is to see you realize yours! I understand the years in the desert. I know what it feels like to have a fire shut up in your bones, knowing that God has something greater for you.

That is why together with my husband Craig Toach, we have trained up our own Fivefold Ministry team and in association with apostles all over the world, we hold in our hands the resources to launch you into your ministry!

Not only do we provide specialized fivefold ministry training, we also provide fivefold ministry assessment, personal mentorship, interactive fellowship with other students and once you qualify - certification, credentials and promotion of your ministry.

Here is What We Offer to Prepare You for Your Fivefold Ministry Calling

By: Colette Toach

Identify Your Fivefold Ministry Calling With Free Evaluation

1. If you have not done so already click on the "evaluation" link above and complete the extensive evaluation.
2. Once you are done click the link to have it evaluated by one of our ministers.
3. From there we will tell you what courses to begin with.

Ministry Certification, Credentials and Ordination

1. To see what program is best suited to you, visit our Degrees page.
2. Temporary credentials are issued to students who have achieved a major in any of our programs
3. Ordination is offered only by the invitation of the Holy Spirit. As a student qualifies in their course of study, we will seek the Lord on their behalf of their readiness to be released into ministry
4. Ministry credentials are issued to those who are ordained by the laying on of hands of the A.M.I. leadership.

Ministry Training Materials That Are Totally Unique

1. The materials that you will study were received as a result of revelation received directly from the Lord.
2. All ministry training materials are based squarely on the Scriptures.

3. Every principle taught has been proved by being lived out practically in real fivefold ministry experience by bone-fide fivefold ministers.
4. Since the lessons are based on revelation given to the Church right now along with the experience of fivefold ministers all over the world, you will not find these teachings anywhere else.

Fivefold Ministry Training That Affects More Than Your Mind

1. We put an emphasis on the training aspect of our Fivefold Ministry Training. This is not just head knowledge, but wisdom you will live.
2. You will literally live each principle as you learn it.
3. You will become what God called you to be, even if there was no previous evidence of this ministry in you.
4. As a result of additional mentoring you will move from general ministry on to your full Fivefold Ministry Office in a very short space of time.

Student Only Benefits

1. You will be given a Personal Lecturer who will follow you throughout your training. All our lecturers have been personally mentored by Craig and I and hold at least one fivefold ministry office. A lecturer will be allocated to you according to your calling, so that you can be sure that whoever is mentoring you is someone who has gone the way before.
2. Your mentor will be someone who has been along the way and can be there to minister to you, guide you,

pray you through and to track your progress. You will be given their contact information so you can keep in touch with them.

3. You will be able to fellowship with other students at the AMI Campus - a place where all students and lecturers network and fellowship

4. You will be able to get help directly from your lecturers via a special Student Questions Forum

5. Weekly Student Only Chats where our lecturers from around the world train you live - leaving time for questions and hands-on training.

The Way of Dreams & Visions Book with Symbol Dictionary Kit

By Colette Toach

This is the ultimate Dream Kit!

In this kit you are not only getting the teaching you need to understand your dreams and visions, but you are also getting the key to decode them.

Everybody wants to interpret dreams today. However, where is the balance between what the world says and what the Word of God says? You are about to find out that as a believer, there is a

How to Hear the Voice of God

world in the spirit and in the Word that breaks all the boundaries of what you knew - or thought you knew.

This goes beyond dream and vision interpretation, it takes you on a journey into the realm of the spirit.

Did you know that your dreams have a meaning? From the very beginning of time the Lord spoke to His people in dreams and visions. In the New Testament this ability has become even greater and instead of a select few, every single believer has the ability to understand what God is saying to them in their dreams.

However, does this mean you have to wait for a dream to hear God? Not at all - Not only can you increase the amount of prophetic dreams you are having, but you can also learn to receive visions and hear from the Lord at any time.

The Symbol Dictionary included in this kit is one of a kind! Apostle Colette Toach does it again... puts up a standard with an apostolic foundation that you can trust. Refer to this Symbol Dictionary over and over again and find out what God is saying to you in your dreams and visions.

You will refer to this Symbol Dictionary over and over again. You'll never have to look very far for an interpretation again. Simply page through this reference book and get the meaning of the symbols in your dreams and visions.

- Keep it at your bedside and look up what your dream means when you wake up
- Look up symbols on the go or while you're ministering

By: Colette Toach

The Lord is talking to you, but do you know what He is saying? Get your copy of the Dreams and Visions Symbol Dictionary today and find out.

Contacting Us

Go to www.ami-bookshop.com to check out our wide selection of materials.

Do you have any questions about any products?

Contact us at: +1 (760) 466 - 7679
(8am to 5pm California Time, Weekdays Only)

E-mail Address: admin@ami-bookshop.com

Postal Address:

A.M.I

5663 Balboa Ave #416

San Diego, CA 92111, USA

AMI Bookshop – It's not Just Knowledge, It's **Living Knowledge**

How to Hear the Voice of God

Made in the USA
San Bernardino, CA
28 November 2015